A PHOTO-LOCATION GUIDEBOOK

PHOTOGRAPHING
DORSET

JURASSIC COAST • PURBECK • RURAL DORSET

MARK BAUER

PHOTOGRAPHING **DORSET**

BY MARK BAUER

First published in the United Kingdom in 2016 by fotoVUE.
www.fotovue.com

Copyright © fotoVUE Limited 2016.
Text and Photography: Copyright © Mark Bauer 2016.
Foreword Copyright © Tony Bates MBE 2016.

Editors: Stuart Holmes and Mick Ryan, fotoVUE Ltd.
Layout, Photo Editor; Stuart Holmes
Book design by fotoVUE and Mountain Creative
Cover design by Nathan Ryder – Vertebrate Publishing.

All maps within this publication were produced by Don Williams of Bute Cartographics.
Map location overlay and graphics by Mick Ryan.
Maps contain Ordnance Survey data © Crown copyright and database right 2016.

A CIP catalogue record for this book is available from the British Library.

ISBN 978-0-9929051-4-9
10 9 8 7 6 5 4 3 2 1

Front cover: *Corfe Castle and the rising sun. September. Canon 5D Mk III, 24-105mm f/4L at 40mm, ISO 100, 1/8 second at f/16, LEE 0.9 soft grad.*
Inside rear flap photo: *Mark Bauer self portrait.*
Rear cover left: *Warm glow of evening light on Durdle Door.*
Rear cover right: *Sturminster Newton mill, and the River Stour on a summer morning.*
Photo opposite: *Marshwood Vale.*

Printed and bound in Europe by Latitude Press Ltd.

For miles around, the Dorset hills rolled and billowed,
like a shaken-out blanket settling on to a bed…
It was beautiful beyond words, one of those rare moments
when life seems perfect.

From Notes from a Small Island
by Bill Bryson

CONTENTS

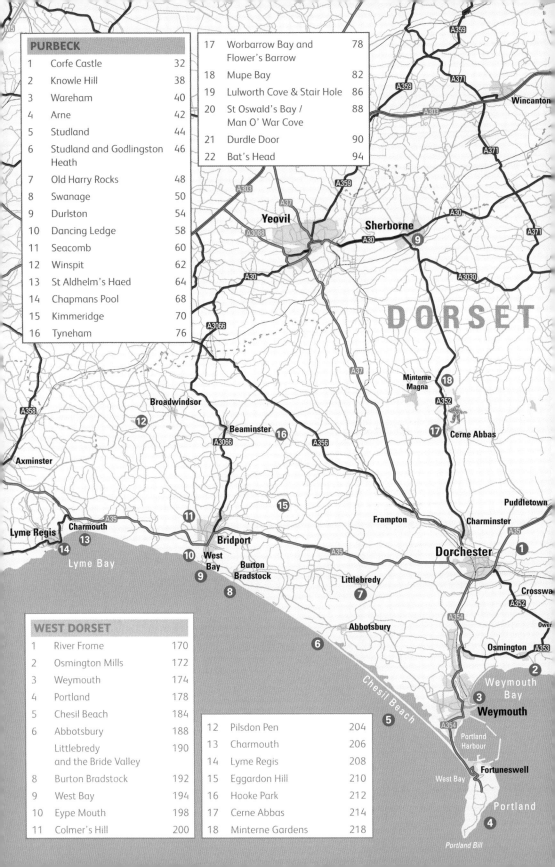

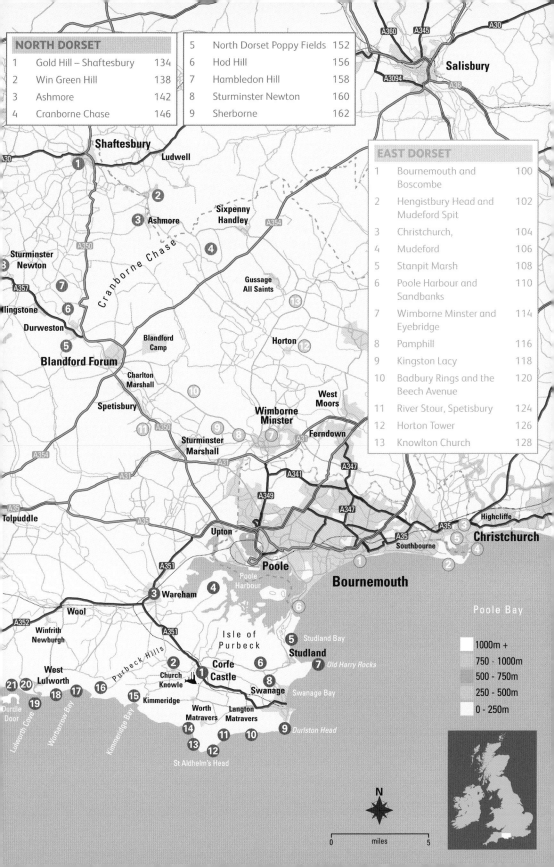

NORTH DORSET

1	Gold Hill – Shaftesbury	134
2	Win Green Hill	138
3	Ashmore	142
4	Cranborne Chase	146
5	North Dorset Poppy Fields	152
6	Hod Hill	156
7	Hambledon Hill	158
8	Sturminster Newton	160
9	Sherborne	162

EAST DORSET

1	Bournemouth and Boscombe	100
2	Hengistbury Head and Mudeford Spit	102
3	Christchurch,	104
4	Mudeford	106
5	Stanpit Marsh	108
6	Poole Harbour and Sandbanks	110
7	Wimborne Minster and Eyebridge	114
8	Pamphill	116
9	Kingston Lacy	118
10	Badbury Rings and the Beech Avenue	120
11	River Stour, Spetisbury	124
12	Horton Tower	126
13	Knowlton Church	128

Poole Bay

1000m +
750 - 1000m
500 - 750m
250 - 500m
0 - 250m

N

0   miles   5

Flowering gorse makes an attractive foreground for Corfe Castle in mid-April.
Canon 5D Mk III, 24-105mm f/4L at 28mm, ISO 100, 1/5 second
at f/16, LEE 0.9 soft grad

Acknowledgements

Being the spouse or partner of a landscape photographer is no easy task. By necessity, landscape photographers work anti-social hours, often getting up in the middle of the night to get ready for a dawn shoot and despite our best efforts, somehow managing to wake up the entire household in the process; or dashing out to catch the sunset, just as the rest of the family are settling down to dinner.

Even more annoying are the times when, having made a decision to stay at home, we then spend an entire evening gazing forlornly at the wonderful light in the distance, clearly manufactured by the gods to taunt us for being lazy.

And of course, landscape photographers are never satisfied. There is always either too much cloud, not enough cloud, or the wrong sort of cloud; not enough mist or the wrong type of mist; the sea is either too rough or too calm and the colour never seems to spread across the sky to precisely where we want it. When I return from a shoot, I'm sure my wife dreads asking the question, 'How was it?' because the most enthusiastic reply she can usually expect is, 'It was OK, but…'

So my biggest thanks have to go to my long-suffering wife Julie, who somehow manages to put up with all of this and also to our son Harry, who tolerates my frequent and sometimes long absences.

Writing is hard work and only comes naturally to a select few. For the rest of us, it is, frankly, a very painful process and if you're a photographer it has to be fitted in around all your other commitments such as commissioned photography and workshops. And just when you think it's all over, then come the rounds of corrections, amendments and additions. Mick and Stuart from fotoVUE have somehow managed to keep me motivated throughout this process, and have been incredibly encouraging and supportive – thanks guys!

Mark Bauer
November 2016

DORSET

Foreword by Tony Bates MBE

Dorset is much loved for the character and scenic beauty of its coast and countryside. The geological strata of the Jurassic period which run diagonally across England from the north east converge within Dorset and outcrop along the coast. This has not only created the dramatic coastline, which justifiably has World Heritage Site status, but is the reason for the beautiful landscape.

Along Dorset's coast from Lyme Regis and past Portland to Hengitsbury Head one comes across a superb variety of scenery which provides a great backdrop along which the South West coast footpath runs.

Inland, away from the conurbation of Bournemouth and Poole, Dorset is largely rural and reflects not only the diversity of the underlying geology but also the influence of man's working of the land over the past 3000 years or more.

It is not surprising that there are many books that illustrate the beauty of Dorset, but this one is different. Mark Bauer has not only provided us with a superb range of photographs but we are provided with great detail on how to find the best viewpoints for ourselves.

As a photographer myself I appreciate the need to look for good conditions to take pictures and Mark suggests the best seasons and times of day to get the best lighting conditions. In addition there are instructions on photographic technique which I am sure will help many visiting photographers.

I have lived and worked in Dorset for 40 years and am very aware the importance of conservation of the countryside and wildlife of this unique county, much of which has been lost since the Second World War. The county however retains much beauty and Mark's photographs certainly do justice to this.

I am sure you will find this book a most valuable companion that will help you capture your own special moments.

Tony Bates MBE
President of the Dorset Wildlife Trust
November 2016

Opposite: Charmouth, looking east from Golden Cap (p. 206) in late summer sunshine. Canon 5Ds, 16-35mm f/4L at 28mm, ISO 100, 1/25 sec at f/11, polariser

Introduction

Dorset is home to what are considered some of the most iconic and photogenic locations in the UK: the extraordinary rock arch at Durdle Door, the 17-mile shingle spit of Chesil Beach and the golden cliffs at Burton Bradstock to name a few. It is world famous for the Jurassic Coast – the first wholly natural World Heritage Site to be designated in the United Kingdom – which makes up all but a few miles of its coastline.

The county is therefore extremely popular with photographers, but there is so much more to Dorset than these classic viewpoints. There are many hidden gems, from beautiful, rarely-visited coves to serene riverside views and the rolling hills of Thomas Hardy's Wessex. It is not a particularly large county, with an area of just 1,024 square miles and being just 60 miles across, but it packs a lot of variety into a small space. Whether you like dramatic coastal views, moorland, hills or woodland, you will find somewhere that inspires you.

I have lived in and been photographing Dorset for over 20 years and I am still discovering 'new' locations, as well as different compositions at places I've visited scores of times. Most of these locations are shared in this book and I hope you find it a useful guide when exploring the area.

There is a danger with a book of this nature that it can encourage something of a 'collector' mentality among photographers, who find themselves following well-worn paths to tripod holes where they can set up their cameras in order to capture a well known composition. While I've included directions to many popular viewpoints, I hope that users of this book will look beyond the obvious and use my suggestions as a springboard for their own creativity. Whilst conditions are always different at a given location and no two photographs are exactly the same, it is much more satisfying to create original compositions than copy something you've seen elsewhere.

I hope you enjoy this book and, more importantly, enjoy photographing this great county.

Mark Bauer
Dorset, November 2016

*Boats on the River Frome at Wareham on a misty September morning.
Canon 5Ds, 70-300 at 207mm, ISO 100, 1/8 sec at f/11*

The view over Chesil Bank from Portland Heights at dusk.
Nikon Df, 24-120mm at 58mm, ISO 200, 2 seconds at f/11

Getting to and around Dorset

Despite being a popular destination Dorset is not as well connected as one might hope. There is no motorway in Dorset and the main roads in the county can get very busy and traffic jams are common especially at peak times and school holidays.

But Dorset is worth the effort and if you avoid peak periods you're unlikely to encounter any problems.

From the North

Go south either on the M1 or M6 and then the M40. The A34 will then connect you to the M3 and then the M27. This does not go all the way into Dorset but finishes in Hampshire, just inside the New Forest National Park, where it goes down to two lanes and becomes the A31. At busy times, this will result in queues.

From the A31 you can then either head down to the coast at Bournemouth or Poole, or continue to join the A35 and head to west Dorset.

Alternatively, for west Dorset follow the M5 from Birmingham then take the A303 and A37.

Winter sunrise at St Oswald's Bay. Canon 5D Mk II, Zeiss 21mm, ISO 100, 46 seconds at f/22, LEE Little Stopper & 0.9 soft grad

From London and the East

From London take the M3 followed by the M27 then the A31 into Dorset. If you are coming from beyond London, then you will most likely use the M25 which connects with the M3.

From the West

The A30 is the main road through the West Country and this joins with the A35 at Honiton in Devon. From here you can follow the A35 into and across Dorset. From further south in Devon or Cornwall, the A38 connects with the A30.

Distances and driving times to Dorchester

Postcode: DT1 1HX	GPS: 50.71116, -2.441181
OS Grid reference:	SY 689 902
London via M3 and M27:	130 miles, 2 hours 45 minutes
Birmingham via M5:	170 miles, 3 hours 7 minutes
Manchester via M5:	249 miles, 4 hours 28 minutes
Newcastle via M5:	377 miles, 6 hours 10 minutes
Glasgow via M6 & M5:	453 miles, 7 hours 20 minutes
Plymouth via A38 and A35:	98 miles, 2 hours

Travelling around Dorset

There is no motorway in Dorset so travelling around the area in high season can take longer than expected. This is made worse by the absence of much dual carriageway. The main east-west road across the county, the A35, is mostly single carriageway with just the odd stretch of dual carriageway. Where two lanes go down into one, such as when approaching Dorchester from the east, bottlenecks can result.

Country lanes can be narrow and winding so be cautious if you are unfamiliar with the roads. Drive slowly; you can find yourself approaching another vehicle head on and will need to be able to stop or pull over safely.

Be considerate to those wishing to travel faster than yourself and allow them to pass.

Animals on the Road

While driving on Dorset's rural roads be prepared for animals on the road. Deer are common and will often be on the roadside, or even in the road, especially around dusk and dawn. Badgers and foxes are also common.

Peak Times

It's not just photographers who like Dorset, it's a very popular area with holidaymakers. In the summer and school holidays roads can get very busy, especially near coastal destinations. This also means that at peak times

Sunrise at Handfast Point near Swanage, mid-April.
Canon 5Ds, Sigma 20mm, ISO 100, 60 secs at f/11, LEE Little Stopper & 0.9 medium grad

at some locations it can be difficult to get shots which are free of people. Planning your journey so that you arrive on location early or late in the day is a good idea and, happily, these times coincide with the best times for photography.

Dorset is much quieter outside of the summer and school holidays, and especially on weekdays.

Train

There are three rail routes running through Dorset:

1. The main line running through Dorset is from London Waterloo to Weymouth and is operated by South West Trains. Cross-Country Trains also operate on this line as far as Bournemouth. They run hourly through services from Newcastle and Manchester and intermediate stations.

2. In North Dorset, South West Trains provide a regular service from London Waterloo to Gillingham, Templecombe and Sherborne which continues to Exeter.

3. A third line runs from Bristol to Dorchester and Weymouth approximately every two hours on weekdays. This is known as "The Heart of Wessex" line and is operated by Great Western Railway.

There is a steam train from Norden Park and Ride to Corfe Castle and Swanage that runs from Easter to the end of October. Recent funding has been allocated to allow the operation of a regular diesel train from Wareham to Swanage, expected to begin running some time in 2017. In theory, this means there will then be regular trains from London Waterloo to Swanage.

Bus

National Express provides long-distance coach services to Dorset. The main Dorset hub is the Bournemouth Travel Interchange next to the railway station.

There is a regular bus service in the main towns and also between towns. In the Bournemouth-Poole-Christchurch conurbation the main operators are More (Wilts and Dorset) and Yellow Buses. In the rural areas the main bus companies are Damory Coaches, More Bus Company and First Dorset.

By Air

Dorset's airport is Bournemouth Airport, which is situated at Hurn, near Christchurch.

Spring is the season for sunshine and showers. Rainbow over Swanage Bay.
Canon 5D Mk II, 24-105mm at 40mm, ISO 100, 20 seconds at f/22, LEE 4-stop ND & polariser

Dorset Weather and Seasonal Highlights

"The storm starts, when the drops start dropping. When the drops stop dropping then the storm starts stopping." (Dr. Seuss)

Thanks to its position on the South Coast, Dorset's climate is one of warm summers and mild winters. It is the third most southerly county in the UK and far less affected by the powerful Atlantic winds than Cornwall and Devon to the west. The entire South West has higher average winter temperatures than the rest of the UK and Dorset has higher summer temperatures than Cornwall and Devon.

Along with Hampshire, Sussex and Kent, Dorset benefits from more sunshine than anywhere else in the country, with over 1500 hours of sun a year. Dorset receives less rainfall than Devon and Cornwall, but more than the counties to the east. It is drier on the coast (800mm rain pa) compared to the chalk downland (1,250mm rain pa) in the centre of the county.

Winter sunrise at Durdle Door. Canon 5D Mk II, 24-105mm f/L at 24mm, ISO 100, 4 seconds at f/22, LEE 3-stop ND

When is the best time to visit Dorset?

Spring – March, April, May

Early spring can be one of the hardest times of year to photograph. During March and most of April the trees are still bare, but with Dorset's mild climate frosts at this time of year are rare. Locations can often be dull and muddy without the mood and atmosphere that winter can bring. April is well-known for showers and sun, and these changeable conditions can mean excellent light and often rainbows; the drama created as a shower clears and the light bursts through the clouds is hard to beat.

April can be a misty season, so getting up high for shots of places such as Corfe Castle and Colmer's Hill is also worthwhile. Morning mist isn't always easy to predict – check the weather forecast and look for clear and cold still nights.

At the end of April into May it is time to head to the woods – Hooke Park, Pamphill and the Beech Avenue near Kingston Lacy – as they return to leaf, and bluebells and wild garlic start to flower.

From mid-May agricultural areas start to become colourful as rape seed begins to flower. Head for the countryside to find both wild and cultivated flowers.

Poppies in the fields above Durweston. Canon 5D Mk II, Zeiss 18mm, ISO 100, 1/10 second at f/11, LEE 0.6 ND grad, polariser

Below: Wild garlic in the wood at Handfast Point, near Studland. Fuji X-Pro2, 10-24mm f/4, ISO 400, 1/20 sec at f/11, polariser

Summer – June, July, August

Summer in Dorset is popular but traditionally it is regarded as one of the least productive times for landscape photography. Foliage loses its freshness and starts to look a little tired, air quality suffers and there can be a lot of atmospheric haze. To create further difficulties the sun is higher in the sky, meaning that for large parts of the day the light can be harsh and un-photogenic. Dawn and dusk become key times for photography, but with sunrise and sunset times of around 5am and 9.20pm in June it's easy to see why many people don't bother. There are, however, still plenty of opportunities for photography at this time of year.

In the summer months the sun rises and sets over the land on the south coast so, as a general rule, this is the time to head inland. Happily, this coincides with some interesting seasonal activity in these areas. June and July see poppies bloom in farmers' fields; a carpet of red stretching out into the distance is a spectacular sight.

On the coast, a few bays and coves are east or west-facing and therefore make good sunrise and sunset locations. Swanage Bay, for example, faces east and, just around the corner, Old Harry Rocks photographs well at dawn all year round. The eastern ledges at Kimmeridge work well at sunset, as do Emmett's Hill and Portland.

Wild flowers can add interest to cliff edges and thrift makes an appearance on some headlands.

Towards the end of August the landscape can look a little bleached, but this is the time of year that colour starts to reappear as the heather starts to flower. Studland and Godlingston Heath, Arne and Pilsdon Pen become covered in a carpet of purple.

As autumn approaches overnight temperatures drop and additional moisture in the air means that this can be a good time for mist in the early mornings, so keep an eye on the forecast and look out for the signs.

Dorset Weather and Seasonal Highlights

Autumn – September, October, November

Autumn brings shorter days, misty mornings and colourful foliage; a favourite time for many photographers. There is often an Indian summer in the early autumn, so sunrise and sunset opportunities are very good, especially on the coast as the sun is now rising and setting over the sea in many locations. The majority of summer holidaymakers have left, meaning that coastal locations are easier to photograph.

Late October and early November are typically the best time for autumn leaves. In Dorset there are good options, with locations such as the Kingston Lacy Beech Avenue and the West Dorset woodlands providing excellent subject matter. This is a good time to photograph the Jurassic Coast as the sun is in an ideal position for both dawn and dusk, with the weather somewhat more clement than in the winter.

Opposite: Wild flowers at Handfast Point, near Studland. Summer. Canon 1Ds Mk II, 17-40mm f/4 at 19mm, ISO 100, 2 seconds at f/16, LEE 0.6 hard grad & polariser

Autumn mist near Corfe Castle. Canon 5D MkII, 24-105mm f/4L at 105mm, ISO 100, 1/125 second at f/11

Autumn touches the beech trees at Kingston Lacy. Canon 5Ds, 70-300mm at 160mm, ISO 200, 13 seconds at f/16, polariser

Winter – December, January, February

While some photographers pack away their kit for the winter and concentrate on catching up with processing images and researching locations for the spring, those in the know get on with taking photographs. Winter is arguably the most photogenic season. The quality of light is excellent, with low sun throughout the day and the air, without the summer's higher levels of moisture, often having fantastic clarity.

Coastal photography is always a good bet, with deserted beaches and stormy seas adding drama. Inland, with trees stripped bare, the landscape has a minimalist appearance in which you can fully focus on the shape and texture of the landscape itself. Away from the coast, there is the chance of frost, which further simplifies scenes by helping to hide distracting elements and softening light by acting like a giant reflector.

Snow isn't common in Dorset but there is a higher chance of it away from the coast and on higher ground. On the rare occasions that it does snow by the coast it's worth making the effort to get out early before it is trampled. Familiar locations can look very different. Listen to the local news and travel bulletins to make sure you can travel to a location safely.

Autumn on the River Stour near Wimborne. Canon 1Ds Mk II, 70-200mm f/4L at 145mm, ISO 100, 1/13 second at f/16

Dorset Weather and Seasonal Highlights

Preparing for the weather

Don't let bad or dynamic weather deter you from using your camera; it's often when the best photos are taken.

Protect your camera

There are simple, cost effective ways to protect your camera if it isn't equipped with its own weather-proofing. Large zip-loc bags and tape or rubber bands work but it can get a bit cumbersome. Disposable rain hoods are basically a plastic bag that is shaped to fit over your camera. They are cheap and effective.

Protect yourself

Waterproof materials such as Goretex and equivalents are expensive but handle pretty much everything the weather can throw at them. Waterproof footwear also makes life more bearable in the rain and when it's wet underfoot. Wellington boots are ideal for wet countryside and coastline photography. A good umbrella is worth carrying, golf umbrellas are ideal but can be difficult to control in windy conditions.

Checklist

- Check the forecast the day before you go out and again in the morning to help with location choice.
- Look at wind strength and direction as this will have a big impact at coastal locations.
- Check tide tables if you are heading to the coast.
- Protect your camera with a dry bag or plastic bag.
- Bring a chamois leather to dry your lens.
- Wrap up well, pack waterproofs and bring a hot drink and food.
- Pack wellies and umbrella just in case.
- Changeable weather can be great for photography
- Focus on the effects of weather: puddles, raindrops, people with umbrellas, wind shields on beaches, wind blowing the vegetation works well with a slow shutter speed.

Local Weather Forecasts

1. Met Office Mountain Weather Forecast
www.metoffice.gov.uk/public/weather/mountain-forecast

2. BBC Weather – Coast and Sea
www.bbc.co.uk/weather/coast_and_sea

3. Local Radio
BBC Radio Solent in East Dorset 96.1FM and 999AM
In West Dorset 103.8FM and 1359AM
Wessex FM 96 and 97.2

Dorset Webcams

1. Swanage Railway webcam – shows Corfe castle:
www.swanagerailway.co.uk/corfe-castle

2. Weymouth Harbour webcam:
www.dorsetforyou.gov.uk/article/423507/Weymouth-Harbour-Masters-Office-Webcam

3. Weymouth beach webcam:
www.dorsetforyou.gov.uk/webcam/weymouthbeach

4. Lyme Regis webcam:
www.lymeregis.org/webcam.aspx

5. Bournmouth Pier webcam:
www.sortedsurfshop.co.uk/webcam_bournemouth

Winter afterglow, Mupe Ledges. Canon 5D Mk III, 16-35mm at 16mm, ISO 100, 60 secs at f/11, LEE 3-stop ND and 0.6 hard grad

The displays of thrift on Dorset cliff tops can be very pretty as this view of Kimmeridge shows.
Canon 5D Mk II, Zeiss 21mm f/2.8, ISO 100, 6 seconds at f/16, LEE 4-stop ND and polariser.

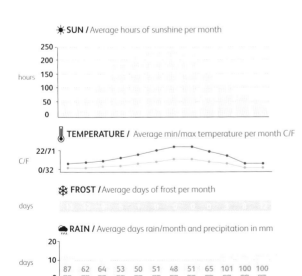

☀ SUN / Average hours of sunshine per month

🌡 TEMPERATURE / Average min/max temperature per month C/F

❄ FROST / Average days of frost per month

☁ RAIN / Average days rain/month and precipitation in mm

Jan	Feb	Mar	Apr	May	Jun	Jul	Aug	Sep	Oct	Nov	Dec
87 mm	62 mm	64 mm	53 mm	50 mm	51 mm	48 mm	51 mm	65 mm	101 mm	100 mm	100 mm

Met Office weather station averages

Met Office weather at Bournmouth Airport
Location: 50.779, -1.835
Altitude: 10 m above mean sea level

Left image opposite page: Colourful heather and gorse
at Pilsdon Pen, in the light of a late summer sunrise.
Canon 5Ds, 16-35mm f/4L at 21mm, ISO 100,
1/5 second at f/11, LEE 0.9 medium grad

Using this Guidebook to Get the Best Images

PURBECK

EAST DORSET

NORTH DORSET

WEST DORSET

Great photographs require being in the right place at the right time regardless of whether you are using a digital, film or mobile phone camera. This is what fotoVUE photo-location guidebooks are about – giving you the information and the inspiration to get to great locations in the best photographic conditions.

In the Right Place

Each location entry in this guide describes a place where you can take great photographs. Comprehensive directions are given, including co-ordinates to the nearest car park or lay-by, nearest postal codes for sat navs and smart phones, and an OS map co-ordinate.

Before you set off for a location study a map so that you know where you are going and give yourself plenty of time to get to your destination. Also read the **accessibility** notes to check the distances and terrain to the location's photographic **viewpoints**.

Maps

For the best detail, recommended maps for Dorset are the OS Explorer Maps (scale 1:25 000).

More affordable and covering larger areas, but less detailed, are the OS Landranger maps (scale 1:50 000).

If you are an occasional visitor you may find the OS Tour maps (scale 1:100 000) to Dorset, Somerset East, Bath & Bristol adequate.

More details at *www.ordnancesurvey.co.uk* and online maps at Google and Bing.

At the Right Time

Great photographs usually depend on light and colour. In each location chapter are detailed notes on the best time of year and day to visit a location to get the best photographic results. Good light can occur any time, however, and often the best times to visit any location is when conditions are rapidly changing, like after a storm.

The topography, sun position and the weather determine how the light falls on the land. Use the sun position compass on the front flap of this guidebook for sunrise and sunset times, to find out where the sun rises and sets on the compass (it changes throughout the year) and sun elevation (how high the sun rises in the sky).

Useful websites for this include *suncalc.org* and the Photographer's Ephemeris.

EXIF data on photograph captions

Included in each photo caption is the shooting information. This is taken from the EXIF data recorded in the file alongside each digital photograph taken. EXIF is short for Exchangeable Image File and records a whole host of information about the settings and equipment used to take that photo including shutter speed, aperture, ISO, date and time the image was taken, white balance, and a list of other parameters.

Light conditions and camera exposure vary but hopefully knowing the settings used for all of these photographs will help your own photography.

Responsible Photography

Minimise your impact by following the Country Code: stick to footpaths, close gates, don't climb over fences and don't leave litter. Resist the urge to bend the rules just for a photo; the more people that trample flowers or climb fences, the more restrictions will come into play.

Other Photographers

At some locations you will encounter other photographers. Be courteous and considerate and stay behind them if they are composing a photograph. If someone arrives after you and the light has just been amazing, resist the temptation to tell them that they have just missed the best light ('you should have been here half an hour ago…')

Self Exploration

The interpretation of viewpoints is entirely down to prevailing conditions and your skill as a photographer.

This guidebook will help you get to some of the best photographic locations in Dorset. The list is by no means exhaustive; use it as a springboard to discover your own photo locations. There are of course many other great places in the area, both known or still waiting to be discovered and photographed. Study a map and look for locations or just follow your nose when conditions are good and discover your own.

Upload your own Dorset Photographs
and Viewpoints at:

www.fotovue.com

Purbeck – Introduction

For many visitors Purbeck is Dorset and it is easy to see why. Purbeck is packed full of beautiful and famous locations such as Old Harry Rocks, Durdle Door, Lulworth Cove, Kimmeridge Bay and Corfe Castle. The world famous 'Jurassic Coast', England's first natural World Heritage Site, has its starting point just outside Swanage at Old Harry Rocks and stretches all the way along the Dorset coast into East Devon. The 96-mile long Purbeck section is arguably the most picturesque stretch.

The Isle of Purbeck – a peninsula rather than a true island – has its eastern boundary along the coast at Studland and is bordered to the north by Poole Harbour and the flood plains of the river Frome. The western boundary is less certain, but most likely placed at the western edge of Worbarrow Bay.

Purbeck is well-known for its geology and is home to some spectacular cliffs and landforms, many of which are highly photogenic. The area has been quarried over the years, which has also led to some interesting photographic opportunities in places such as Dancing Ledge and Seacombe. Many of the local buildings are made from Purbeck stone, which was also used extensively in the rebuilding of London after the Great Fire.

A large part of the area is a designated Area of Outstanding Natural Beauty with some of the coast owned by the Ministry of Defence. The area was first requisitioned during World War II for training exercises in preparation for the D-Day landings and is still used as a training area today, with live firing taking place on the ranges. Tyneham is now a ghost village and it and the surrounding area are only accessible at weekends and holidays. Check access when planning trips, see notes on p.80.

Although there have been objections to the MOD's ownership of the land, it does mean that there has been no development and the area has therefore become a haven for wildlife. There is definitely a wonderful 'away from it all' feeling when walking across the ranges.

The 'classic' view of Durdle Door from the beach, with the warm glow of the evening sun and a rainbow to set it off. Canon 5D Mk III, 16-35mm f/2.8 at 21mm, ISO 125, 2.5 seconds at f/11

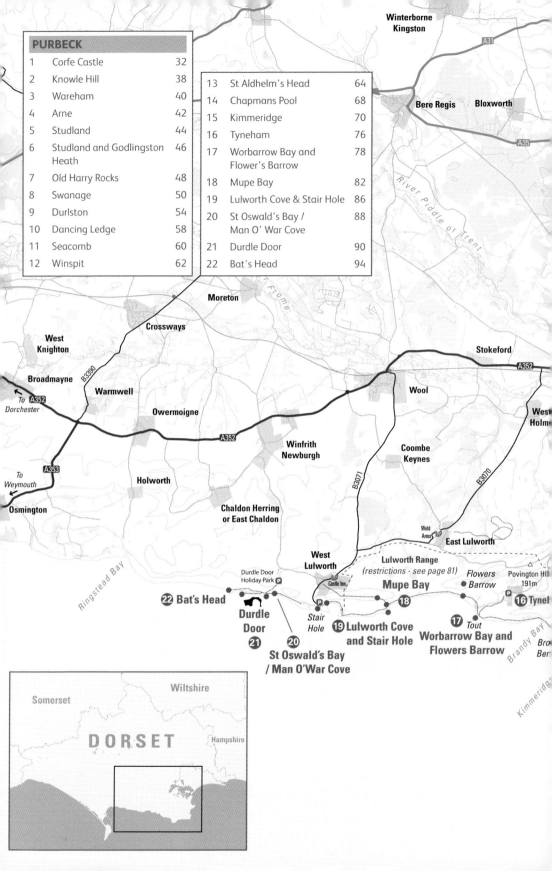

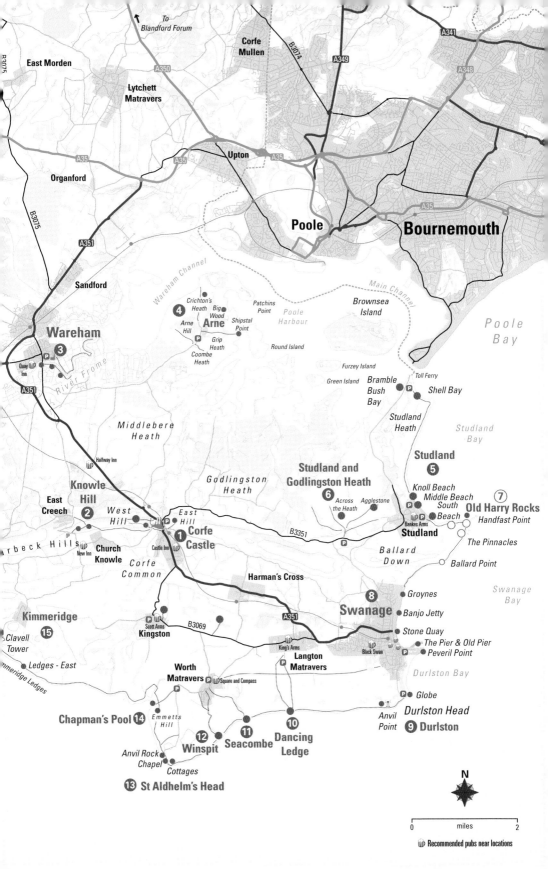

A misty September sunrise from West Hill.
Canon 5D Mk III, 24-105mm at 40mm, ISO 100, 1/40 sec at f/9

Corfe Castle was built by William the Conqueror to defend the only gap in the Purbeck Hills for 11 miles. This imposing structure must have struck terror into the hearts of any attacking army. The castle finally fell during the English Civil War when a group of Parliamentarians entered with their coats worn inside-out so that they resembled Royalists. Once inside, they turned their coats the correct way and there began a simultaneous attack from outside and within. This event is supposedly the origin of the phrase 'turncoat'. Later that year, Parliament voted to demolish the castle, resulting in its ruined appearance today.

Parliament did modern photographers a great favour; the romantic ruin probably photographs better than any perfectly-preserved castle, especially on misty mornings when the ruins rise above the top layer of mist like a scene from a fantasy film. It's not obligatory to shoot it in these conditions, though this seems to be the shot that everyone wants to get. The classic viewpoint is from West Hill but if you want your shots to stand out from the crowd there are other high vantage points you can explore.

What To Shoot and Viewpoints

Viewpoint 1 – West Hill

From the National Trust car park on the A351, cross the road and near the junction with Tyneham Road, go through a gate into a field. Cross the field, passing a barn on your left and go through a gate on the far side. Follow the footpath up West Hill. It's a steep climb, but how far up you go is entirely up to you – there are good viewpoints from quite low down. If there is a mist, you may need to climb quite far to get above it. Mist behind the castle really helps it stand out. Lower down the hill, the castle will break the horizon, thus being separated from the background and this can be a better option if there is no mist behind the castle.

Viewpoint 2 – West Hill from the other side

Alternatively, drive or walk along Tyneham Road for a couple of hundred metres. There is a lay-by on the left, just past the bridge and almost opposite this there is a gate through to the hill. A set of steps are carved into the hill, but although it's slightly easier underfoot, it's just as steep a climb. This alternative viewpoint works very well later in the day, when attractive side-lighting can hit the castle.

Viewpoint 3 – From Kingston

Drive through Corfe Castle towards Swanage and turn right immediately after leaving the village. Drive up the hill and turn right into Kingston at the Scott Arms pub. Park (legally and considerately) in the village then walk out of the village towards Swanage, east on the B3069. Just past a converted church on the left, climb over a stile into a field. Follow the footpath for thirty metres to panoramic views across Corfe Common towards the castle. A 70-200mm lens is recommended for this viewpoint, which shows the castle commanding the gap in the hills.

*Opposite: VP4. The castle viewed from across Corfe Common
Canon 5D Mk II, 70-200mm f/4 at 200mm, ISO 100, 1/8 sec at f/16*

*Above: Late afternoon in autumn from West Hill (Viewpoint 2)
Canon 5D Mk II, 24-105mm f/4 at 31mm, ISO 100, 2.5 secs at f/22*

Above: VP3. Corfe Castle from Kingston. Canon 5D Mk II, 70-200mm f/4 at 145mm, ISO 200, 1/80 sec at f/8

Corfe Castle backlit in mist on an October morning. Canon 5Ds, 70-300mm f/4-5.6L at 78mm, ISO 100, 1/800 second at f/8

How To Get Here

From Wareham follow the A351 towards Corfe Castle. The National Trust visitor centre and car park is just past the 30mph sign on the left. Alternatively, almost opposite the visitor centre, you can turn right into Tyneham Road where there is a large lay-by on the right.

Parking Lat/Long: 50.642057, -2.058855
Parking Postcode: BH20 5DR
Parking OS map co-ordinate: SY 959 824
Map: OS Explorer Map OL15 (1:25 000) Purbeck and South Dorset

Accessibility

From the car park to the foot of West Hill is 250m. It is a steep climb to the top and you may want to pause for breath along the way. There's no need to climb all the way to the top as there are good views from various points lower down. There is no wheelchair access. Kingston is a short drive from Corfe Castle and the viewpoint is a short, easy walk from the village. An alternative is to photograph it from the beer garden of the Scott Arms – wheelchair access is possible. The viewpoint across the Common is about 2 km from Kingston along the footpath, but not wheelchair-friendly.

Best Time of Year/Day

Corfe Castle photographs well at any time of year but for mist, spring and early autumn – especially April and late September – are best. Mist can occur at any time of the year so don't write off the summer months. Whilst the castle looks good at any time of day, it is at its most atmospheric first thing in the morning.

Viewpoint 4 – Across the Common

From Kingston continue along the B3069, towards Langton Matravers and Swanage. Between the first and second turnings on the right, towards Worth Matravers, there is a lay-by on the right. Park here. After one hundred metres or so there is a bridleway on the left through farmland, which you can follow all the way back to Corfe Castle village. From various points along here, there are views across the Common towards the castle. Again, what is interesting about this viewpoint is that it shows the reason for the situation of the castle.

Viewpoint 5 – East Hill

From the National Trust car park, walk towards the village. As the main road bears round to the right, take the minor road to the left. Pass under the railway bridge and you will see a footpath on your left leading up the hill.

This is a less popular viewpoint than West Hill because the castle is harder to separate from its background and it has a less pleasing shape from this angle, but it can work well at sunset.

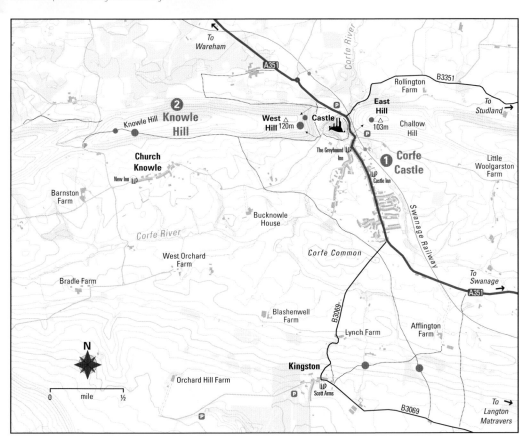

The best known views of Corfe Castle are from West Hill and having made the effort to climb up there it would be a shame not to walk west along the ridge to get to Knowle Hill. From here there are far-reaching views across the Purbeck Valley in one direction and over to Poole Harbour in the other. On mornings when it's too foggy to see Corfe Castle, Knowle Hill is often above the fog giving views of the tree tops and hills rising above the mist in the Purbeck Valley or looking north towards central Dorset.

What to shoot and Viewpoints

You can either walk along the ridge from West Hill (see page 34) or from the parking spot at the western end of Knowle Hill where you go through the gate behind you and follow the footpath along the ridge. Walking along the ridge from either direction you will see wonderful views opening up in front of you.

Viewpoint 1 – Towards Poole Harbour from the Eastern End of the Knowle Hill

From the eastern end of the ridge you can shoot north over Norden and Hartland Moor towards Poole Harbour. This is long lens territory – anything from the full-frame equivalent of 200-400mm. Compositions from here look especially good on a misty morning where telephoto lenses 'compress' the layers in the landscape.

Viewpoint 2 – The Purbeck Valley from the Eastern End of the Knowle Hill

Without moving very far from Viewpoint 1 you can get very different, but equally good compositions in the other direction including overlapping hills, copses and the church at Kingston. Again, longer focal lengths work well, especially on misty mornings, but neither is a must for successful shots of this viewpoint.

Viewpoint 3 – Looking north from the Western End of Knowle Hill

From further along Knowle Hill you can shoot over Furzebrook towards Wareham and central Dorset. Spring and autumn mists are not uncommon, giving a primeval atmosphere to the woodland below.

Viewpoint 4 – The Purbeck Valley from the Western End of Knowle Hill

There are fine views of the Purbeck Valley from this end of the hill too, especially with early morning light raking across the fields. St James' Church at Kingston is also visible from here and St Peter's Church in Church Knowle also makes a good focal point for a composition.

Snow in the Purbeck Valley photographed from the eastern end of Knowle Hill. Canon 5D Mk II, 70-200mm f/4 at 94mm, ISO 100, 0.3 second at f/16

A low-lying mist over Hartland Moor with Poole Harbour in the background.
Olympus OM-D E-M5 45-200mm f/4-5.6 at 200mm, ISO 200, 1/50th second at f/11

How To Get Here

Knowle Hill is a mile to the west of Corfe Castle and about 3.5 miles south of Wareham. You can get to it by walking west along the ridge from West Hill (see page 34) or you can access it from the western end via Church Knowle. To get to the western side, turn into Tyneham Road, almost opposite the Corfe Castle visitor centre on the A351. Continue along this road until you get to the village of Church Knowle. Take the first right immediately past the village and drive up a fairly steep hill. Just where the road bends sharply to the right at the top of the hill you will see a small lay-by directly ahead, in front of a gate. Be considerate when parking and allow access to the gate for farm vehicles.

Parking Lat/Long: 50.638411, -2.100293
Parking Postcode: BH20 5NT
OS map co-ordinate: SY 930 820

Map: OS Explorer Map OL15 (1:25 000) Purbeck and South Dorset

Accessibility

Approached from the east, it's a steep walk up West Hill, but this allows you to then walk along the ridge, combining a shoot at Corfe Castle with one at Knowle Hill. Access is much easier from the western end of the hill, where it is a much gentler slope, though disabled access is still not possible.

Best Time of Year/Day

The views towards Poole Harbour look best at sunrise, especially when there is a glow on the horizon and mist on Hartland Moor. The Purbeck Valley is at its best early in the morning, when the light first reaches over the hills. Spring and autumn will give you the best chance of a misty morning.

Wareham is an historic market town situated on the River Frome. Originally the site of a small Roman settlement, the town as we know it was founded by the Saxons. Remains of the ramparts, built to defend the town against the Danes, were likely built by Alfred the Great and still exist along with the churches of Lady St Mary and St Martin.

Most of the photographic interest in Wareham is located on or near the River Frome. A winter morning walk along the towpath can give some magical compositions.

VP1. A wider view from the bridge showing the quay on the left. Fuji X-E1, 10-24mm at 16mm, ISO 200, 0.4 sec at f/11

What To Shoot and Viewpoints

Viewpoint 1 – From the Bridge

Turn left out of the car park and walk the few metres onto the bridge. There are several different compositions looking east along the river. The natural tendency is to put on a long lens and zoom in on the boats moored in the river. This can work especially well when there is a little early morning mist and some backlighting to create a romantic atmosphere. Wider angle shots are also effective, with the Old Granary framing the view on the left and the floodplains on the right.

Viewpoint 2 – Lady St Mary Church

Cross the bridge and walk along the towpath for a couple of minutes. Across the river you will see the garden of the Priory Hotel with the church behind it. On a still day, try using reeds for foreground interest or reflections in the river, using a moderate wide angle.

Viewpoint 3 – Along the Towpath

Walk the towpath. The views change throughout the year, as reeds come and go and boats moor up in different locations. You may find that you have to work harder to get good compositions along here as it's not always easy to get enough elevation to get separation between the foreground and subject. If you have a very tall tripod available this would be the place to use it – don't worry about the extra weight, it's a short, level walk. Using live view, especially if your camera has an articulated screen, can help when composing shots at awkward angles.

*Opposite: VP1. Summer sunrise from the bridge.
Canon 5Ds, 70-200mm f/4 with 2x converter,
at 308mm, ISO 100, 1/20th second at f/11*

How To Get Here

From Poole head towards Dorchester on the A35 and turn onto the A351 at the Baker's Arms roundabout.If coming from Dorchester follow the A352 direct to Wareham. Pass through Sandford and follow the signs into Wareham town centre. Drive through the town along North Street, and as you reach the outskirts, just past the library, turn left into the quayside car park by the Old Granary.

Parking Lat/Long: 50.684133, -2.109385
Parking Postcode: BH20 4LP
OS map co-ordinate: SY 923 871

Map: OS Explorer Map OL15 (1:25 000) Purbeck and South Dorset

Accessibility

This is a very accessible location next to a road. The towpath is suitable for wheelchairs, although from a wheelchair you may not be able to see over the sides of the bridge of Viewpoint 1.

Best Time of Year/Day

Winter is a lovely time of year for photographing along the towpath, especially if the reeds and grasses on the banks of the river are frosty. Sunrise is the best time for shooting along the river from Viewpoint 1, but other times of day also work well for shots from the towpath.

The Arne peninsula juts out into Poole Harbour opposite Poole and is probably best known for its RSPB reserve. There are plenty of species to keep enthusiastic birdwatchers happy including Dartford warblers, nightjars, avocets, little egrets and even the occasional migrating osprey. There are other types of wildlife, too, with 22 species of dragonfly, sand lizards, smooth snakes and sika deer.

Even if you're not into wildlife photography, this Site of Special Scientific Interest (SSSI) has plenty to offer with expanses of open heathland, the heather flowering from mid to late August, old oak woodland and fabulous views of Poole Harbour.

What to Shoot and Viewpoints

Viewpoint 1 – Shipstal Point

Take the right hand fork at the church and keep going straight ahead along this track for about a kilometre until you reach a footpath branching off on the right. Continue until you reach Shipstal Point, with views along the Wych Channel and across Poole Harbour to Brownsea Island. At the right time of year there is plenty of heather to use as foreground interest in these views or to be photographed as a subject in its own right.

Viewpoint 2 – Woodland

There is oak woodland at Arne which gives options for colourful shots in autumn or fresh greens in spring. With a light mist in the morning, you may be able to shoot sun beams through the branches of the trees.

Viewpoint 3 – Wildlife

There is a large herd of sika deer on the reserve. These are not native to the UK but have become naturalised and live on the heath and woodland at Arne. Fans of smaller creatures will find plenty of insects, in particular dragon flies as well as several species of reptile, including sand lizards in the heathland. Last but not least there are many different species of birds. Keep an eye on the RSPB website for recent sightings and other information: *www.rspb.org.uk/Arne*

A sika deer in the heather at Arne. © Ross Hoddinott. Nikon D300, 70-200mm f/2.8 at 200mm, ISO 200, 1/320 second at f/4.0

Early morning light on the heather at Shipstal Point. Canon 5D II, 18mm f/3.5, ISO 100, 2.5 seconds at f/16

How To Get Here

Arne is 3 miles east of Wareham. From Wareham take the B3075 towards Stoborough. Just past the King's Arms pub turn left into Nutcrack Lane which then becomes Arne Road at the hamlet of Ridge. From here it's a further 2.5 miles until you see the car park on your right. If visiting for a dawn shoot, the car park may be locked. If so there is some limited on-street parking by the church slightly further on.

Parking Lat/Long: 50.689891, -2.041138
Parking Postcode: BH20 5BJ
OS map co-ordinate: SY 971 878

Map: OS Explorer Map OL15 (1:25 000) Purbeck and South Dorset

Accessibility

Most of the walking is fairly level on good footpaths, though there is no proper disabled access. The main viewpoints are 1–2 km from the car park.

Best Time of Year/Day

Early mornings work well at Arne, for both landscape and wildlife photography. There is interest throughout the year, though mid to late August is best for heather. October is deer rutting season and sand lizards have their best colour in April.

Sand lizard in the heathland. © Ross Hoddinott. Nikon D300, 150mm f/2.8 macro, ISO 200, 1/640 second at f/4.5

Studland is a pretty coastal village on the north-eastern tip of the Isle of Purbeck and is the first stop if you've arrived via the Sandbanks ferry. It is famous for its naturist beach and for being a regular haunt of children's author Enid Blyton – several of her novels were set in the area.

There are three beaches, owned and managed by the National Trust: Knoll Beach, Middle Beach and South Beach, all offering good views towards Handfast Point and Old Harry Rocks. Nearby Bramble Bush Bay also has excellent views over to Brownsea Island.

What to Shoot and Viewpoints

Viewpoint 1 – Old Harry Rocks from Knoll and Middle Beaches

A very short walk from the National Trust car parks are Middle Beach and Knoll Beach. The views to Old Harry look best at sunrise shooting towards the colour. There is little foreground here, on Knoll beach there is a concrete slipway which works well when waves crash over it, and

July sunrise from the dunes at Knoll Beach. Canon 5Ds, 16-35mm at 24mm, ISO 100, 1/4 sec at f/16, Lee 0.9 medium grad.

there is a small stream which can be used as a lead-in. Otherwise, shoot at low tide and try to use the reflected colour in the wet sand, or if you are lucky, the retreating tide may have left ripples in the sand. Further back, there are sand dunes with heather which flowers for a couple of weeks from mid-August.

Viewpoint 2 – Old Harry from South Beach

Walk along the shore towards South Beach from the National Trust car park at Middle Beach. Where Middle Beach transitions to South Beach rocky ledges are exposed at low tide and there are some interesting rock pools; experiment with different camera heights to make the most of the reflections. It can be slippery underfoot.

Viewpoint 3 – A close view of Old Harry Rocks

Once or twice a year it is possible to walk from South Beach to the base of Old Harry Rocks. The opportunity arises when there is a 'perigean spring tide.' This is when the moon is new or full and closest to Earth and coincides with a spring tide. You will get a unique viewpoint and be able to photograph the rock stack known as 'Old Harry's Wife' which is not visible from the cliff-top viewpoint (see Old Harry Rocks p. 48). However, great care must be taken; check and double check the tide times and heights and make sure you leave enough time to return safely. Do not do this walk alone and let someone know when you expect to be back. The shore is very slippery so wear suitable footwear. Park in the National Trust car park next to the Bankes Arms and walk down to South Beach. Allow 45-60 minutes to reach Old Harry.

Viewpoint 4 – Shell Bay

This is the stretch of beach nearest the ferry. There are good views towards Poole and Bournemouth that are best shot at the beginning of the day. Sand dunes and marram grass can provide good foregrounds. If you like human interest in your shots, this is a popular spot with early morning walkers.

Summer sunrise from Middle Beach, looking towards Old Harry. Canon 5D Mk II, 24-105mm f/4 at 24mm. ISO 100, 80 secs at f/16

Old Harry (middle stack) and his Wife from the foreshore.
Canon 5D Mk III, 16-35mm f/2.8 at 16mm, ISO 100, 0.3 sec at f/16

How To Get Here

From Corfe Castle take the B3351 east for 5 miles. For the Middle
Beach car park turn right in the village immediately past the post
office, into Beach Road and to the car park. For the Knoll Beach car
park go through the village. The entrance to the car park is on the
right, just past the Knoll House Hotel on the left. Continue along
Ferry Road to get to the Shell Bay car park.

From the Sandbanks Ferry the Shell Bay car park is on the left,
immediately past the toll booth. The Knoll Beach car park is on the
left just before the village and for the Middle Beach car park take
the first turning on the left as you enter the village.

Parking Lat/Long: 50.645623, -1.951257
Parking Postcode: BH19 3AX
Parking OS map co-ordinate: SZ 035 828

Map: OS Explorer Map OL15 (1:25 000) Purbeck and South Dorset

Accessibility

Access to the beach from the Middle Beach car park is down a few
steps and takes just a couple of minutes. To the beach from Knoll
Beach and Shell Beach car parks is a short, level walk. The ledges
between Middle Beach and South Beach can be very slippery.

Best Time of Year/Day

The view towards Old Harry from Studland's beaches works especially
well at sunrise and in the early morning. Any time of year works well,
though in mid-winter the sun rises over the headland, which will be
silhouetted. Later in the year there is more directional side-lighting
onto Old Harry and the headland. The beaches generally look their
best at low tide. The prevailing wind is south-westerly, but after an
easterly you may find that a lot of seaweed has been washed up
on to the beach spoiling its otherwise clean look. The view towards
Brownsea from Bramble Bush Bay works well at most times of day.

Right: Shell Bay sunrise.
Canon 5D, 17-40mm f/4 at 17mm, ISO 100, 1/10 sec at f/22

Partially enclosing the village of Studland to the north and west is the nature reserve of Studland and Godlingston Heath. Owned by the National Trust, it is the largest surviving expanse of lowland heath in Dorset. It has international importance for its habitats of sand dunes, peat bogs, heathland and a freshwater lagoon. All six species of British reptile are found here.

There are fine views across Poole Harbour and the gentle hills are a real reminder of what Thomas Hardy's Wessex would have looked like. In the middle of the heath and offering some of the best views is the Agglestone, a 400-ton lump of ironstone. Local legend says it was thrown there by the devil who was sitting on the Needles on the Isle of Wight when he saw Corfe Castle being built. Upset by the building he threw his cap at it, but it fell short and became the Agglestone.

What to Shoot and Viewpoints

Viewpoint 1 – The Agglestone

A 10-minute walk along the footpath from the lay-by brings you to the Agglestone. There are several possible compositions: close up, using the footpath to lead in to the shot and also more distant views, from higher up and with Poole Harbour as a backdrop.

Viewpoint 2 – Across the Heath

Follow the footpath from the lay-by. The first section takes you through the Purbeck Golf Course. Just past this, there are good options for shots to the north and north west across the heath. In late summer this is an impressive carpet of purple heather.

A close view of the Agglestone in evening light. Canon 5D Mk II, Zeiss 21mm, ISO 400, 1/6 sec at f/11, LEE 0.6 hard grad, polariser

Common or Viviparous Lizard. © Ross Hoddinott. Nikon D70, 150 Sigma macro, ISO 200, 1/200th at f/11

Viewpoint 3 – Reptiles

March to May are good times to look for reptiles. With night times still relatively cool, cold-blooded reptiles need to spend long periods of time basking in the open to raise their body temperatures.

How To Get Here

Studland and Godlingston Heath is just outside Studland and can be accessed from the village; there are various footpaths. The easiest way to get to the Agglestone is to drive out of the village towards Corfe Castle. Keep right when the road forks (the left fork takes you down towards Swanage) and after half a mile there is a small lay-by on the right. If you reach the Purbeck Golf Club you have gone too far. The footpath from here takes you across the golf course, take care there are golfers playing, and is signposted to the Agglestone.

Parking Lat/Long: 50.636620, -1.9771287
Parking Postcode: BH19 3AA
OS map co-ordinate: SZ 017 818

Map: OS Explorer Map OL15 (1:25 000) Purbeck and South Dorset

Accessibility

The footpaths across the heath are fairly even. It is a moderate slope down to the the Agglestone and back up – an easy to moderate walk. There is no wheelchair access.

Refreshments are available at the Bankes Arms in Studland and there are toilets at Knoll Beach.

Best Time of Year/Day

The heather flowers in late August and this is probably the best time for landscape photography. The purple heather really adds something to pictures of the Agglestone in particular. It's possible to get shots throughout the day, but early morning works well for shots of the heath, especially if there is a mist. For the Agglestone the angle of the sun is good in the evening but sunrise shots can also work well.

For photographing reptiles the best time is on warm, early spring days when they emerge from hibernation to look for a mate. Male sand lizards turn bright green to attract females.

Opposite: A misty morning on the heath in late August. Canon 5D Mk II, Zeiss 21mm, ISO 100, 1 sec at f/16, LEE 0.6 hard grad

Old Harry Rocks are a set of chalk stacks at Handfast Point on the Purbeck coast between Studland and Swanage. Originally part of a chalk ridge which stretched across to the Isle of Wight, this has been gradually eroded by the sea leaving the slightly more resistant rock of the stacks. Erosion continues and stacks such as Old Harry will eventually collapse, as happened to Old Harry's Wife in 1896.

The origin of Old Harry's name is uncertain; some say it is a nickname for the Devil, others that the rocks were named after Harry Payne, a pirate from Poole, who stored his contraband nearby.

The chalk stacks are an impressive sight, especially in the warm light of a rising sun. There are many possible compositions, including shooting in the opposite direction towards Swanage towards another group of stacks known as the Pinnacles.

What to Shoot and Viewpoints

From the car park walk down the road with The Bankes Arms pub on your right. At the bottom of the hill turn left onto the footpath past the public toilets. Keep on this footpath for 20-30 minutes until you reach the top of Handfast Point. The main viewpoints are within a few metres of each other. Please take care when photographing from all of these spots and keep away from the edges of the cliffs as they are unstable and you can never be sure if you are standing on an overhang.

Viewpoint 1 – Old Harry

Looking north towards Bournemouth and Poole, you will see Old Harry at the end of what remains of the chalk ridge. When composing shots, try to position yourself so that there is a reasonable degree of separation between the cliffs and Old Harry. There are possibilities for both including foreground interest, or going for a more

The Pinnacles from Handfast Point at sunrise, early autumn.
Canon 5D Mk III, 16-35mm f/2.8 at 17mm, ISO 200, 62 secs at f/22

minimalist approach; the former works well in spring and early summer when there are wild flowers growing on the cliff top and the latter is best when there is a strong sky.

Viewpoint 2 – St Lucas' Leap

The remains of an old footpath runs along the top of the ridge and makes a nice 'vanishing point' composition. The gap in the ridge is known as St Lucas' Leap –supposedly named after a greyhound which leapt do its death while chasing a hare.

Viewpoint 3 – The Pinnacles

Look in the opposite direction from Old Harry towards Swanage and you will see the Pinnacles, another group of chalk stacks. The central stack is a dramatic triangular shape. Compositionally the options are similar to shooting Old Harry; make sure there is enough separation between the Pinnacles and the cliffs and, depending on conditions, you can choose to shoot with or without foreground. Both landscape and portrait work here.

Viewpoint 4 – The Pinnacles from the South

Walk along the cliff path towards Swanage for a few hundred metres and there is a view of the Pinnacles to the north. It's possible to use the sweep of the cliff edge as a leading line, but take great care in this spot as there have been some serious landslips in recent years.

A spring morning looking towards the Pinnacles from the south.
Canon 5D Mk II, 24-105mm f/4 at 24mm, ISO 100, 203 secs at f/11

Above: Spring sunrise, Old Harry Rocks (Viewpoint 1).
Canon 5D Mk II, Zeiss 18mm f/3.5, ISO 100, 13 secs at f/22

How To Get Here

From Corfe Castle take the B3351 east for 5 miles to Studland and when in the village turn right at the post office into School Lane. Turn left into Watery Lane and follow the road as it bends left and uphill past the Bankes Arms. Park in the National Trust car park next to the pub. The Bankes Arms is a great place to stop for lunch after a shoot with fabulous views over Studland Bay towards Old Harry.

If coming via Sandbanks Ferry you will approach Studland from the other direction. Turn left at the post office into School Lane.

Parking Lat/Long: 50.642281, -1.948435
Parking Postcode: BH19 3AU
OS map co-ordinate: SZ 053 824

Map: OS Explorer Map OL15 (1:25 000) Purbeck and South Dorset

Accessibility

The walk to Handfast Point from the car park is a fairly gentle slope and takes 20-30 minutes. There is no wheelchair access, but there are some views towards Old Harry from the garden of the Bankes Arms pub. The footpath can be muddy in winter. When planning a visit check the wind speed on the weather forecast; Handfast Point is exposed with high cliffs, not the best place be in strong gusts.

Best Time of Year/Day

This works well at all times of year and most times of day. It's especially good at sunrise in winter; the chalk cliffs will be side lit revealing their wonderful texture. In summer the sun rises just to the right of Old Harry as viewed from the cliff top. High tide is best as the base of the cliffs and stacks can look a little messy during a very low tide. Old Harry Rocks is popular and can get busy during the summer, especially at weekends. In summer it's best to go at the beginning or end of the day.

Right: Looking along the old footpath towards St Lucas' Leap.
Canon 5D II, Zeiss 18mm f/3.5, ISO 100, 241 secs at f/11

The seaside town of Swanage is characterised by its Victorian architecture and has a wonderfully old-fashioned vibe. For a trip back to the 1970's go and watch a film in the local cinema. The town has an Enid Blyton connection and was the inspiration for Toytown in the Noddy books. Swanage is the fictional home town of one of British television's greatest comic creations, Basil Fawlty.

In recent years Swanage has become popular with photographers due partly to its proximity to the Jurassic Coast. It is also very photogenic in its own right. Along the beach there are wooden groynes and groyne markers, a concrete jetty and a Victorian pier with a pagoda-shaped shelter. From the pier you can shoot the remains of the original pier which is now one of the most photographed subjects on the south coast of England. The pier is especially popular with fans of long exposure minimalism.

A winter sunrise over the Banjo Jetty. Canon 5D Mk II, 17-40mm f/4 at 19mm, ISO 100, 24 seconds at f/16

What To Shoot and Viewpoints

From the car park it is a couple of minutes walk down to the pier where you can then walk along the seafront, stopping at various viewpoints along the way.

Early morning, looking towards the town from the beach. Canon 5D Mk II, Zeiss 21mm f/2.8, ISO 100, 6 seconds at f/22

Viewpoint 1 – Peveril Point

Easy to ignore, this small headland is behind the pier as viewed from Broad Road car park. The easiest way to get here is simply to walk to the far end end of the car park and then walk along Peveril Point Road. From Peveril Point you can shoot across the bay towards Ballard Down and Old Harry Rocks, or back towards the town, with the slightly out-of-place Wellington Clock Tower as a focal point in the frame.

Above: The Old Pier on a winter morning, framed to exclude the new pier on the left and Peveril Point on the right. A little time was spent with the clone tool to remove some buoys. Canon 5D Mk II, 24-105mm at 28mm, ISO 200, 300 seconds at f/11

Viewpoint 2 – The Pier

There are many options for shooting the new pier. You can make the most of the angles and symmetry, use the railings to lead into the shot and use the hut at the end of a pier as a focal point. Low viewpoints work very well as there are commemorative plaques on the deck which make great foregrounds, if you can get enough depth of field. The pier is privately owned and maintained by a charitable trust and receives no funding from the local town council. A small entry fee is charged to help with upkeep and the pier is usually only open during daylight hours – sometimes a little later during the summer. Check their website to confirm opening times when planning a shoot: ***www.swanagepiertrust.com***

A long exposure of the stone quay. Canon 5D Mk II, 24-105mm f/4 at 60mm, ISO 200, 182 seconds at f/11

Viewpoint 3 – The Old Pier

Although it's become something of a cliché, the wooden posts which are the remains of the old pier are still a wonderful subject, especially for long exposures. You can shoot from the concrete section of the pier behind the diving school and either juxtapose the old and new piers in your composition, or isolate the old pier from its surroundings to add a sense of mystery and romance. Alternatively, shoot it from further along the pier with Peveril Point and the Spanish-style apartments behind. Be aware that for about six months of the year the diving school erects an unsightly plastic pontoon around the old pier which makes getting a good shot rather problematic. There is no definite time for its being set up and dismantled, it depends on the weather conditions. To be on the safe side plan to shoot between mid-November and the beginning of April.

Viewpoint 4 – The Stone Quay

This is another viewpoint for those who enjoy minimalism and long exposures, the stone quay features a harbour wall which can either be isolated in the frame or shot with the headland of Ballard Down in the background as a counterpoint. The concrete slipway between the quay and the pier also has a lot of potential. The open air restaurant on the quay (seasonal opening hours) is also a great place to stop for refreshments.

Viewpoint 5 – The Banjo Jetty

The 'banjo jetty' (so called because of its shape) is halfway along the promenade, opposite Victoria Avenue. A modern, concrete structure, which is part of the town's flood defences, it is not an immediately obvious subject but has appeal for those who like bold, structural compositions. It's a natural candidate for symmetry, but it's worth trying other approaches as well. For something different try a daytime exposure of 1–2 seconds when visitors are walking up and down and record as ghostly blurs in the frame.

Viewpoint 6 – Groynes

There are wooden groynes along the beach which make excellent subjects. The favourites being those with red 'baskets' (groyne markers) on the end. There are many compositions which work well; try isolating them from their surroundings or using ND filters for long exposures. Centring the groynes in the frame and shooting straight out to sea is another creative option; good to try on overcast days or for monochrome conversions. Don't overlook using the sea defences as foreground interest with the town or Ballard Down in the background. At the far end of the beach, by the Bull and Boat restaurant, there is a marker post sticking up out of the sand – a natural candidate for a minimalist shot at high tide.

Viewpoint 7 – Swanage Bay from Ballard Down

If you walk or drive out of town towards the ferry along Ulwell Road there is a large lay-by on the right, just past the Village Inn. From here there is a footpath up to Ballard Down. It is quite a steep climb but not too far and worth it for the views over Swanage Bay. It is also possible to continue along the coast path to Old Harry and then Studland.

Opposite top: Summer's evening on Swanage Pier; the low viewpoint makes the plaques loom large in the frame. Canon 5D MkII, 17-40mm f/4 at 17mm, ISO 100, 5 secs at f/22

Opposite right: A winter sunset from Peveril Point. The distinctive Wellington Clock Tower is just to the left of centre. Canon 5D, 17-40 at 22mm, ISO 100, 2.5 secs at f/16

View over Swanage Bay from Ballard Down, autumn afternoon. Canon 1Ds Mk II, 24-105mm f/4 at 24mm, ISO 100, 0.6 sec at f/16

How To Get Here

There are two ways into Swanage: from Wareham, follow the A351 through Corfe Castle and then into Swanage, or take the Sandbanks Ferry, and then take the left fork just past Studland. Once in Swanage, go through town towards the pier, turn right up Seymer Road and turn left into Broad Road car park. There are other long stay car parks in town, but this is the closest to the pier.

Parking Lat/Long: 50.606707, -1.952845
Parking Postcode: BH19 2AR
OS map co-ordinate: SZ 031 791

Map: OS Explorer Map OL15 (1:25 000) Purbeck and South Dorset

Accessibility

The route along the seafront is level, easy and suitable for wheelchair users. For those unable to get onto the beach, it is possible to shoot from the promenade. Most of the pier is also wheelchair-friendly, though there are steps up to the final section with the shelter. The walk up to Ballard Down is steep and requires a moderate level of fitness and wheelchair access is not possible.

Best Time of Year/Day

Swanage is an east-facing bay and benefits from good sunrises all year round. There are not really any sunset opportunities, but it does photograph well during the day and the pier and old pier are excellent 'grey day' options. Swanage is a very popular tourist resort and generally speaking, it does get very crowded during the summer and is pretty busy from Easter through till October. At these times, it is best to concentrate on early morning photography – at least it should be warm and sunny.

Common Blue butterflies. © Ross Hoddinott.
Nikon D800E, 200mm f/4, ISO 400, 1/200 sec at f/11

Durlston Country Park, owned by Dorset County Council, is a 280-acre nature reserve and Site of Special Scientific Interest located just south of Swanage. It is a haven for wildlife with over 250 species of birds, 33 species of butterfly, thousands of other invertebrates and 578 recorded species of flowering plant. Purbeck stone was quarried here in the 19th and 20th centuries. Remains of an old quarry can be seen at Tilly Whim Caves, a well-known local landmark. Local entrepreneur, George Burt, built the 'Castle' at Durlston Head in 1887. It now houses exhibitions, a restaurant and a visitor centre.

For those more interested in landscape there are good views along the coast as well as some interesting features such as the Durlston Globe (also commissioned by Burt) with its 1880s map of the world, and the lighthouse at Anvil Point.

What to Shoot and Viewpoints

Viewpoint 1 – The Globe

The Globe is behind the castle, a short walk from the car park. Measuring three metres in diameter it is a slightly incongruous sight, overlooking the sea. It's definitely worth a shot or two though, and from here and the coast path around it, there are views over Durlston Bay and Swanage Bay towards Ballard Down and Old Harry Rocks. With a telephoto, you can juxtapose the two headlands or you can go wider and include the footpath in the foreground.

Viewpoint 2 – The Lighthouse

Continue south west on the coast path for about a kilometre and you will reach Anvil Point Lighthouse.

It shoots well from all sides; from the elevated positions around it there are some interesting foregrounds, including dry stone walls. Closer views also work well.

Viewpoint 3 – Wildflowers

It's not possible to list all of the wildflowers present at Durlston, but it is well known for orchids, spider orchids in particular. April is generally the best time to visit, but keep an eye on their website; it is frequently updated with information about current flora and fauna: *www.durlston.co.uk*. There is a field of cowslips that flower in late spring, usually around May, very near the Castle.

Viewpoint 4 – Wildlife

There is an abundance of wildlife at Durlston. As well as sea birds, peregrine falcons have been known to nest in the cliffs. Again, the website is a useful source of up to date information with the latest sightings listed. There are some interesting species of butterfly, including blues and skippers and in common with other parts of Purbeck, you can also see reptiles, including adders.

How To Get Here

From the lower High Street in Swanage, near the pier, walk or drive up either Seymer Road or Park Road, both of which lead into Durlston Road. Follow Durlston Road into the park and car park. Alternatively, you can walk up to Durlston along the south west coast path from Peveril Point.

Parking Lat/Long: 50.595722, -1.9547135
Parking Postcode: BH19 2JL
Durlston OS map co-ordinate: SZ 033 772

Map: OS Explorer Map OL15 (1:25 000) Purbeck and South Dorset

Accessibility

There are many paths around the park, covering a wide range of terrain. The route to the lighthouse is via a tarmac path, but does involve a steep climb back up to Durlston Castle and the car park. There are several marked walks – the Wildlife Trail and the Woodland Trail are short (2km and 1 km respectively) but there is some uneven ground.

Off-road mobility buggies ('trampers') or an off-road wheelchair are available to hire for visitors with mobility problems.

Best Time of Year/Day

Regarding flora and fauna, there is interest all year round and detailed information is given on the Durlston Country Park website: *www.durlston.co.uk/wildlife-and-marine.aspx*

For views of the Globe and from the cliff top back towards Swanage and Ballard Down, sunrise shots are possible all year round as the cliff is east-facing. The lighthouse is best shot at sunrise from November to March and at sunset from early November to mid-January.

Anvil Point lighthouse in the warm glow of a December sunset.
Canon 1Ds Mk II, 24-105 at 87mm, ISO 100, 1.6 secs at f/22

Looking over the Globe to Durlston Bay.
Canon 1Ds Mk II, 17-40mm f/4 at 17mm, ISO 100, 1/10 sec at f/16

Cowslips in warm evening light. © Ross Hoddinott.
Nikon D300, 70-200mm f/2.8 plus 2x converter at 400mm, ISO 200, 1/125 sec at f/5.6

Dancing Ledge is the site of an old quarry on the Purbeck coast near Langton Matravers. It gets its name from the patterns the waves sometimes make when they wash over its flat surface. There is a small tidal swimming pool in the ledge which was blasted out of the rock in Victorian times for the use of local school children.

It takes a bit of effort to get here and to reach some of the best spots involves some scrambling, but it's more than worth it. This quiet location has lots of foreground rocks and pools combined with a very dramatic backdrop.

What to Shoot and Viewpoints

From the car park follow the footpath towards Spyway Farm, pass through a gate and cross the first field. Head for the gate at the far end of the second field and follow the path down the steep hill. Climb over the stile at the bottom and walk down to Dancing Ledge. To get down to the ledge itself go to the left side of the cliff where the drop is smallest. You'll need to climb down about five feet or so; don't jump, as you'll land on a very slippery surface.

Viewpoint 1 – From above the Ledge

Before scrambling down onto Dancing Ledge itself it's worth pausing to take a shot or two from the small cliff above it; in fact, if you're not in an agile mood and don't fancy the climb down to the ledge there are more than enough options up here to keep you happy. There are views along the coast to the east and west, plenty of foreground interest, including some rock pools and from the western end you can get a shot including the whole of the ledge, to show it in context.

Viewpoint 2 – The Swimming Pool

Climb down onto the ledge from the eastern end of the cliff – you'll find one spot where the drop is only about five feet and you can lower yourself down carefully. The pool makes an excellent foreground focal point, especially with an incoming tide and waves washing up into it. It photographs well from either end so is a good subject at both sunrise and sunset.

Viewpoint 3 – Looking West

From the western end of the ledge you can shoot across rugged rocks along the cliffs towards Lulworth and Kimmeridge. The edge of the ledge makes useful foreground interest for a wide angle shot and in winter you can shoot the sun as it dips below the horizon out at sea.

Viewpoint 4 – Fossils

There are lots of ammonites in the rocks at Dancing Ledge, some of them quite large. They make good studies in themselves as well as foreground interest for a wider view. A real reminder of why this is known as the Jurassic Coast.

Top left: With the winter sun low in the sky the cliffs at Dancing Ledge take on a golden glow. From the small cliff above the ledge. Canon 5D, 17-40mm f/4 at 17mm, ISO 100, 1/13 sec at f/16

Top right: Winter sunset from the western end of the ledge. Canon 5D Mk III, 16-35mm at 16mm, ISO 100, 77 seconds at f/11

Bottom: Winter sunrise as the waves wash over the tidal swimming pool in the ledge. Canon 5D Mk III, 16-35mm f/2.8 at 16mm, ISO 100, 6 seconds at f/11

How To Get Here

From Swanage, head out of town on the A351 towards Corfe Castle. Just past Swanage School fork off left onto the B3069 to Langton Matravers. Continue past Putlake Adventure Farm on your left into the village. Go past the Post Office and the Kings Arms on your left and a church on the right and turn left into Durnford Drove, with the Scout Hut on the corner. Continue to the end of Durnford Drove where you will find a small car park – don't fork off left to Langton House holiday property. Park here and go through the gate at the far end onto the footpath.

From Corfe Castle, turn right immediately past the village onto the B3069 towards Kingston. At the top of the hill follow the road sharp left with the Scott Arms on your right. Continue along the road until you reach Langton Matravers. Turn right into Durnford Drove.

Parking Lat/Long: 50.604102, -2.004704
Parking Postcode: BH19 3HG
Dancing Ledge OS map co-ordinate: SY 997 768

Map: OS Explorer Map OL15 (1:25 000) Purbeck and South Dorset

Accessibility

This is quite a hard walk, down (and then back up) a steep hill so you need a moderate level of fitness. Unfortunately there is no wheelchair access to Dancing Ledge.

Best Time of Year/Day

Winter is definitely the best time for photography at Dancing Ledge; from early October through untill the end of February the sun rises over the sea and from mid-November until the end of January it sets over the sea. Daytime shots are possible all year round.

Early morning light in winter, looking towards the western cliffs (Viewpoint 3).Pentax 645D, 55mm, ISO 100, 6 seconds at f/22

Seacombe, like Winspit in the next chapter, is one of several old quarries along the coast. It is accessed from the village of Worth Matravers. The walk here is not physically challenging although the footpath across the fields can get muddy in the winter and once here, the descent to sea level is easier than Winspit.

An alternative is to do a circular walk starting at Worth Matravers and walking to Winspit, then along the coast path to Seacombe and back to Worth through the Seacombe Valley.

The character of the cove is very similar to Winspit and images of one might easily be mistaken for the other unless you look carefully. However, it is a wider bay with a slightly wider range of compositional possibilities and moving around is much easier here than at Winspit.

What to Shoot and Viewpoints

From the car park walk down into the village and past the duck pond on your right. Cross the road and you will see the footpath to Seacombe. The footpath takes you through the Seacombe Valley down to the sea at Seacombe Cliff. Although you need to be careful on the descent down to the shore, the path is much less steep and slippery than at Winspit. Once there you will see the rocky ledges stretching out in front of you with the layered cliffs of Portland stone on either side of the bay.

Viewpoint 1 – From the Western Side of the Bay

On the right hand side of the bay as you face the sea there are some jagged rocks and ledges which make excellent foreground for compositions towards the cliffs on the left. This is an excellent option at sunrise with a wide-angle lens.

Viewpoint 2 – The Eastern Cliffs

There are lots of interesting compositions to be found looking across the ledges towards the cliffs on the left. There are some channels eroded into the ledges which make good lead-in lines when the waves surge through them. There are opportunities for 'misty water' shots as the waves run over and between the ledges or you can try shooting the backwash of waves to create texture in the foreground.

Viewpoint 3 – The Western Cliffs

Shooting towards the western cliffs works well at sunset or post-sunrise when the low sun can help to enhance the texture in the cliffs and foreground. If you shoot from near the cliffs on the eastern side of the cove you can try classic 'big foreground' compositions. There are some channels in the ledges which can be used to exploit the movement of the water as waves wash up through them.

How To Get Here

Seacombe is accessed via Worth Matravers, see Winspit.

Parking Lat/Long: 50.598776, -2.038167
Parking Postcode: BH19 3LE
Seacombe OS map co-ordinate: SY 983 765
Map: OS Explorer Map OL15 (1:25 000) Purbeck and South Dorset

Accessibility

The walk to Seacombe is about 1.5 kilometres over easy ground, with one or two moderate hills. It can be very muddy in winter so if you have a pair of wellies which are comfortable to walk in, these would be the best option for footwear. The walk down to the shore is much easier than at neighbouring Winspit although care is still needed. You won't need to do as much scrambling over rocks as at Winspit but the ledges can still be quite slippery. There is no wheelchair access.

If you're doing Winspit and Seacombe as a circular walk starting and finishing at Worth Matravers, pop into the Worth Tea Rooms at the end. The food is excellent and highly recommended.

Best Time of Year/Day

Autumn and winter are the best time of year. From late September through till mid-March the sun rises over the sea. It never completely sets over the sea but in mid-winter is far enough round to create good colour at sunset. Daytime shots are possible all year round.

Opposite: Winter sunrise, towards the eastern cliffs (Viewpoint 2). Canon 5D Mk III, 16-35mm at 20mm, ISO 100, 15 sec at f/16

Winspit is another old quarry in the cliffs along the Purbeck coast. It was a working quarry until the 1950s, producing stone for buildings in London. During the Second World War it was used as a site for naval and air defences. In more recent times, it has seen use as a filming location including the BBC's Dr Who.

Although it's only a short distance from the pretty village of Worth Matravers, Winspit feels remote and wild, with rugged cliffs and threatening jagged rocks. It's one of the few places along this stretch of the coast where big waves really crash onto the shore. The cove is fairly small but, outside of the main holiday season, there's rarely anyone else here.

What to Shoot and Viewpoints

Walk through the village with the church on your right and follow the road around to the right, with the village hall on your left. Turn left down Winspit Road. This is a private road and you will walk past some houses, but it is

a footpath. When you get past the houses climb over the stile and continue along the footpath for about another kilometre until you reach the clifftop above the cove.

From here there are some rough steps down to sea level, but if you don't fancy the climb down there are good views from the cliff top.

Viewpoint 1 – From the Cliff Top

The steps down to the shore are awkward in places and can be quite slippery if it has been raining or if a lot of sea spray has blown onto them. If you decide to be cautious by not descending the steps you won't miss out on good opportunities as there are good compositions to be made from the cliff top, especially from the western side looking across towards Swanage in the east. In fact this can be the best spot to shoot from if you want to convey the power of the waves crashing onto the rocks.

Viewpoint 2 – From the Shore, Looking East

There are some rocks on the foreshore which you will need to climb over – carefully – to get the best views. Depending on the tide height, a wide flat ledge may be revealed. This makes an excellent foreground focal point with the waves washing over it. Try a longer exposure as the water is rushing back out to sea – this can create dynamic lead-in lines. You can shoot from the rocks on the foreshore or if you head to the right-hand side of the cove there is a raised ledge at the base of the cliff which can be a good place to set up. Caution is advised, especially if you decide to walk along this ledge; big waves can wash up onto the ledge and it's not worth risking if the sea is rough. Make sure you know what the tide is doing. The cliffs on the left of the bay are an interesting shape and texture and the rocks and ledge can be used in the foreground to frame a wide angle shot.

Viewpoint 3 – From the Shore, Looking West

From the opposite side of the cove you can photograph towards the south west. In the early morning, the directional light can reveal beautiful texture in the foreground ledge and background cliffs. The ledge itself can make a wonderful lead-in line as it curves around and through the composition.

Looking west along the ledges at Winspit.
Canon 5D Mk II, Zeiss 18mm f/3.5, ISO 100, 15 seconds at f/11

Winter sunrise from across the ledges at Winspit.
Canon 5D Mk II, Zeiss 21mm f/2.8, ISO 100, 5 seconds at f/22

How To Get Here

From Swanage drive out of town along the A351. Just past Herston turn left onto the B3069 through Langton Matravers. Once out of Langton turn left towards Worth Matravers and continue into the village. Take a sharp right just past the Square and Compass pub and you'll find the village car park – please leave money in the honesty box. Alternatively, at quiet times of the day or year you may well find somewhere to park in the village near the duck pond.

Approaching from Wareham drive along the A351 towards Corfe Castle and Swanage. Immediately past Corfe turn right onto the B3069 and go up the hill towards Kingston. At the top follow the road round to the left, with the Scott Arms pub on your right and continue towards Langton Matravers and Swanage. The turning for Worth Matravers will be on your right after about 2 miles.

Parking Lat/Long: 50.598776, -2.038167
Parking Postcode: BH19 3LE
Winspit OS map co-ordinate: SY 976 760

Map: OS Explorer Map OL15 (1:25 000) Purbeck and South Dorset

Accessibility

The walk down to Winspit takes around 20 minutes from the top of Winspit Road and the footpath is very even. Coming back up it's a moderate slope. The climb down to the shore needs caution; the steps are uneven and can be very slippery. Walking poles are useful to help you keep your balance. Once on the shore be very careful of large waves and incoming tides. The rocks on the foreshore are uneven and slippery and the ledge in front of them is very slippery. Wheelchair access is not possible.

Best Time of Year/Day

Having a very similar position, orientation and aspect to Seacombe, the same best times and seasons apply, see previous entry. It is best to visit early in the day between September to mid-March as the sun rises over the sea during this time. The sun never sets directly over the sea but in mid-winter some colour radiates around.

St Aldhelm's Head marks the southern tip of the the Purbeck Peninsula and is another of the area's hidden gems. Here you will find a thirteenth century chapel, a coastguard station and a terrace of coastguard cottages. The Telecommunications Research Establishment at RAF Worth Matavers played an important role in the development of radar during the Second World War. A monument near the coastguard station marks this contribution.

As well as impressive views both east and west, the squat Norman church has a brooding presence, and its location close to the cliff edge can result in some very atmospheric images in the right light. The interior is also worth photographing with its wonderful vaulted ceiling and ancient graffiti carved into the stone work.

Although not far off the beaten track, St Aldhelm's Head has a sense of isolation which can be exploited if you shoot from the right angle.

Winter sunrise at St Aldhelm's Chapel. Canon 5D Mk III, 16-35mm f/2.8 II at 16mm, ISO 100, 1/13 second at f/11

Left: Early morning light, looking west along the coast in mid-September. Pentax 67II, 55mm lens, Fuji Velvia 50

What to Shoot and Viewpoints

St Aldhelm's Head shares a parking and start point with Chapman's Pool, the next location, with which it can be combined in a circular walk. From the car park, follow the footpath for about two kilometres to the chapel and coastguard cottages.

Viewpoint 1 – Exterior of the Chapel

Dramatic, moody lighting suits the chapel best. Clear blue skies do it no justice at all so try to get there when the sun is low in the sky. It doesn't matter which end of the day this is as the building photographs well from several angles. As with all buildings the angle of the sun is important for revealing its depth and 3-D appearance.

There's not much in the way of foreground interest so don't be afraid to place the chapel low in the frame, especially if there is a dramatic sky above. With a wide angle lens this can create quite a bit of distortion so compose wide enough to allow for correcting the verticals during processing. If shooting to the south be aware of the flag pole next to the coastguard station and try to hide it behind the chapel if possible.

The chapel is also an excellent subject for black and white photography, especially infrared. See overleaf.

Viewpoint 2 – Interior of the Chapel

Interior space is limited and it's very dark so give your eyes time to adjust. There are lots of possibilities which work well. The window is to the right of the altar and this can create a problem with contrast as the rest of the building is very dark. Choose angles carefully to avoid this contrast or be prepared to bracket exposures widely to blend together in post processing.

One of the coastguard cottages under a dramatic sunset sky.
Canon 5D Mk II, 24-15mm at 88mm, ISO 100, 181 secs at f/16

Viewpoint 3 – The Coastguard Cottages

If you stand in front of or to the side of the chapel, you can show the coastguard cottages in the wider landscape, which emphasises how isolated they are. There are often cars parked in front of them which can spoil the effect but many of them are holiday lets so if you visit in winter there's a chance they will be vehicle-free.

Viewpoint 4 – Clifftop Views

There are far-reaching views to the east and west which can work well both at sunset and sunrise, depending on the time of year. In late summer and early autumn make use of the long grasses for some foreground interest.

Viewpoint 5 – Anvil Rock

There is a small cliff below the coastguard station where local quarrymen left behind an anvil-shaped pillar of rock as a seamark to aid safe passage through the rough waters of St Alban's Race below. To get there join the coast path at the coastguard station and walk east towards Durlston. After about 250 metres there is a track which forks away from the main path and doubles back towards the west. It slopes gently downwards and takes you past some derelict buildings. You will see Anvil Rock in front of you. There are also some steps to get down here but there is no handrail and they can be slippery.

The landscape here has a very bleak feel to it; the only feature really is Anvil Rock itself. Dramatic, stormy lighting can suit this view, as can long exposures and monochrome conversions.

An infrared shot of the chapel.
Fuji X-E1, 10-24mm at 10mm, ISO 400, 58 seconds at f/11, Hoya IR72 filter

How To Get Here

St Aldhelm's Head is just over a mile south west of Worth Matravers. From Swanage drive out of town along the A351. Just past Herston turn left onto the B3069, through Langton Matravers. Once out of Langton turn left towards Worth Matravers and continue into the village. Drive through the village past the duck pond on your left and past the village hall as the road turns sharply to the right. Continue for about three-quarters of a mile and then take a sharp left just before you get to a barn conversion surrounded by a dry stone wall. Drive along the rough track for about 100m and you will find a small car park.

Approaching from Wareham, drive along the A351 towards Corfe Castle and Swanage. Immediately past Corfe turn right onto the B3069 and go up the hill towards Kingston. At the top follow the road round to the left with the Scott Arms pub on your right and continue towards Langton Matravers and Swanage. The turning for Worth Matravers will be on your right after about 2 miles.

Parking Lat/Long: 50.596525, -2.053090
Parking Postcode: BH19 3LL
St Aldhelm's Head OS map co-ordinate: SY 960 755

Map: OS Explorer Map OL15 (1:25 000) Purbeck and South Dorset

Accessibility

The track to St Aldhelm's Head is a private road belonging to the Renscombe Estate. Although it is possible to drive along the track, vehicular access is only permitted for the coastguard station and cottages. However, it is worth contacting the estate to arrange disabled access by car. On foot it is a mostly level walk of about 2 km. The path is a little rough in places and can get waterlogged in winter so wearing good quality walking boots is advised

Best Time of Year/Day

It's possible to find good angles at St Aldhelm's Head all year round. Early morning and evening will generally provide the most favourable light, although the chapel will look good at any time of day if there is a dramatic sky overhead, and the interior can be photographed at any time.

Opposite: Anvil Rock at sunrise.
Canon 5D Mk II, Zeiss 21mm f/2.8, ISO 100, 170 secs at f/11

Chapman's Pool

Chapman's Pool is a horseshoe-shaped cove just around the corner from St Aldhelm's Head and it's possible to combine the two locations on a circular walk. The cliffs backing the cove are up to 400 feet high with the upper parts composed of fossil-rich Kimmeridge Clay. A fishing hut on the shore used to serve as a lifeboat station in the late 19th century.

Chapman's Pool isn't the easiest place to access, but this has the advantage that there won't be too many people around; a pleasant contrast with the enormously popular Lulworth Cove just a few miles along the coast. Shooting from the cliffs on the eastern side of Emmetts Hill reveals the shape of the cove and cliffs on the far side, and the access is much easier.

What to Shoot and Viewpoints

Go through the gate at the far end of the car park and follow the marked footpath through the field. Climb over a stile at the end of the field and you are on the South West Coast Path. If you turn left onto the path, you will reach Emmetts Hill, with views over Chapman's Pool and you can continue round to St Aldhelm's Head. To get down to Chapman's Pool continue straight ahead. Be warned though, the descent this way is very steep. Alternatively, there is a new path to the right which takes you on a slightly longer but less steep route via the Hill Bottom track.

Viewpoint 1 – Houns-tout Cliff

Once down to the shore walk past the fishermen's huts to where the cove opens out to the sea. Opposite, you will see the distinctive shape of Houns-tout Cliff which makes an excellent background focal point. You will find plenty of rocks on the shore for foreground interest. Although this viewpoint works well during the day, it's an excellent dusk shot, with long exposures giving an ethereal, misty look to the waves washing over the rocks.

Viewpoint 2 – Towards Egmont Point

Stay on the cliff path and walk south along Emmetts Hill. You will see several interesting rocky outcrops on the cliff top; on one in particular resembles a gate and makes useful foreground interest for a sunset shot to the west.

Viewpoint 3 – The Cove from Emmetts Hill

There are several places along the cliff top where you can see the shape of the cove revealed. Use a wide angle lens and look for foreground interest such as wildflowers or rocky outcrops. Aim to use the natural lines of the cliff top and bay to lead the eye around the composition.

Opposite: Summer sunset, looking towards Egmont Point. Canon 5Ds, 16-35mm f/4 at 24mm, ISO 100, 1/50 sec at f/11

How To Get Here

Chapman's Pool is located a mile west of Worth Matravers. From Swanage drive out of town along the A351. Just past Herston turn left onto the B3069 through Langton Matravers. Once out of Langton turn left towards Worth Matravers and continue into the village. Drive through the village past the duck pond on your left and past the village hall as the road turns sharply to the right. Continue for about three-quarters of a mile and then take a sharp left just before you get to a barn conversion surrounded by a dry stone wall. Drive along the rough track for about 100m and you will find a small car park.

Approaching from Wareham drive along the A351 towards Corfe Castle and Swanage. Immediately past Corfe turn right onto the B3069 and go up the hill towards Kingston. At the top follow the road round to the left with the Scott Arms pub on your right and continue towards Langton Matravers and Swanage. The turning for Worth Matravers will be on your right after about 2 miles.

Parking Lat/Long: 50.596525, -2.053090
Parking Postcode: BH19 3LL
Chapman's Pool OS map co-ordinate: SY 955 770

Map: OS Explorer Map OL15 (1:25 000) Purbeck and South Dorset

Accessibility

It's quite a climb down to the sea at Chapman's Pool. If you take the most direct route there is a real danger of slipping and even the less steep route via Hill Bottom is not easy. This is a location where you'll definitely want to take a friend along with you. If in any doubt stick to the cliff-top viewpoints. These involve only a short, level walk – around 1 to 1.5 km – but a certain amount of care is needed: don't stray too close to the cliff edge, as the cliffs are unstable and there have been one or two incidents in recent years. There is no wheelchair access.

Best Time of Year/Day

Chapman's Pool looks best towards the end of the day, whether shot from the shore or the cliff top. From the shore it is best shot in winter when the sun sets over the sea, but the cliff top shots work well in summer when you can shoot towards the setting sun.

September sunset at Clavell's Pier.
Canon 5D Mk III, 16-35mm f/2.8 at 18mm, ISO 100, 15 seconds at f/11, ND

Until the end of the 20th century Kimmeridge Bay was largely undiscovered by photographers, being more popular with fossil hunters, anglers and scuba divers. The main section of the bay is overlooked by Clavell's Tower – a folly built in 1830 by the Reverend John Richards Clavell. By 2006, coastal erosion had left the ruined tower precariously close to the cliff edge and in serious danger of slipping onto the shore below. Before this happened the building was purchased by the Landmark Trust who dismantled the tower then rebuilt it, stone by stone, 25 metres back from the cliff. Work was completed in February 2008 at a cost of around £900,000. The tower is now a holiday let.

With its commanding position on the cliff, Clavell's Tower makes a very effective focal point for compositions. There are plenty of other subjects including rocky ledges, headlands, rock pools, a waterfall, remains of an old stone pier and some fascinating geology, with many fossils visible as you walk over the ledges.

Looking across the central ledge towards Clavell's Tower at dusk.
Canon 5D Mk II, Zeiss 21mm f/2.8, ISO 200, 363 seconds at f/11

What to Shoot and Viewpoints

The bay is directly below the car park. Follow the footpath down to the shore from the right-hand edge of the car park. You can walk around the shore to Broad Bench on the western side and, when the tide is low, to Clavell's Pier and the eastern ledges on the opposite side. If the tide is too high you can get to Clavell's Pier over the top through the car park. Turn right just past the toilet block and go past the fishermen's huts then climb down to the rocky shoreline in the far left corner. You will also pass the steps up to Clavell's Tower and the coast path.

Viewpoint 1 – Clavell's Tower

There are many variations on compositions using the tower as a background focal point: looking across the large central ledge in the bay, using the rock pool in the ledge as foreground interest, using the small boulders on the foreshore as foreground interest or using the smaller ledges on the eastern side of the bay, which are revealed at low tide. If using the larger, central ledge in the shot, a mid-tide of around 0.75m–1.00m works best. Movement in the foreground can really aid compositions, so if there are waves washing over the shore try using a neutral density filter to extend exposure times and capture movement in the water. If you shoot at dusk there is a good chance there will be lights on in the tower as there are often holidaymakers staying there.

Towards Clavell's Tower from the western ledges, September evening. Canon 5Ds, 16-35mm at 19mm, ISO 100, 8 seconds at f/11, LEE Landscape Polariser and 1.2 ND

Viewpoint 2 – The Main Central Ledge

The central ledge makes an interesting subject in itself, especially for fans of minimalism or long exposures. It is possible to isolate the ledge from its surroundings and a wide angle lens can exaggerate the perspective so that it stretches out to sea. This is a good option on overcast days especially if there is some texture in the sky. At sunset the ledge works as foreground for shots towards the headland at Broad Bench.

Viewpoint 3 – The Western Side

The far right side of the bay is home to some interesting geology. Keep your eyes open as you walk along for ammonite fossils underfoot. On the western edge of the bay you'll be standing on golden-coloured ledges, criss-crossed with cracks, that resemble an elephant's hide. Get low to fill the frame with the rock texture or seek out small inlets in the ledges which frame the view towards the far side of the bay.

Viewpoint 4 – Broad Bench

This can only be accessed on holidays and weekends, as it is part of the army ranges. See notes on page 81.

To get to Broad Bench, continue along the shore and around the headland, scrambling over large rocks. Once here you will see that the character of the bay is slightly different again; the ledges are bumpy and textural with large cracks and crevices which get filled by the incoming tide. You will find yourself spoiled for choice when it comes to foreground for shots towards the east and Clavell's Tower.

Viewpoint 5 – Clavell's Pier

The stone pier was destroyed in a storm in 1745 and the remains form a triangular group of rocks, smoothed by the elements. They have a fabulous texture when wet and make excellent long exposure studies with the waves washing over them. The pier probably works best from the eastern side, when shooting towards the west as the headland at Broad Bench provides a strong focal point in the background. Again, a tide height of around 0.75m – 1.00m is ideal, though it's possible to shoot from this spot until the tide is around 1.8m in height.

Viewpoint 6 – The Eastern Ledges

With a tide height of up to around 1m you can carry on past Clavell's Pier and you will find a series of ledges. The lower the tide, the more are revealed, and with very low tides it's possible to walk for quite a long way along this stretch of the coast. Make sure you know what the tide is doing however as there is a danger of getting cut off at high tides. Also, some of the large rocks are less stable than they look. From the ledges there are a variety of compositions looking back towards Clavells Pier and Broad Bench. This is a particularly good option for a sunset shoot in summer when the sun is setting too far over the land for shots of the main part of the bay.

Shooting towards Broad Bench from the eastern ledges is an excellent option at sunset in the summer. Canon 5D Mk III, 16-35mm f/2.8 at 16mm, ISO 100, 30 seconds at f/11

Opposite: A minimalist shot of the central ledge at sunset. Canon 5D Mk II, 24-105mm at 28mm, ISO 100, 340 seconds at f/11

How To Get Here

From the A351 just outside Corfe Castle turn into Tyneham Road, opposite the B3351. After about 1.5 miles, you will pass through the village of Church Knowle. After a further 1.5 miles turn left, signposted towards Kimmeridge. The road twists and turns up and down a hill for a mile or so until you reach Kimmeridge village. Drive through the village with Clavell's Café on the left (an excellent place to stop for a lunch or a snack) until you reach the entrance to the bay. Stop at the toll booth to pay for parking then continue on to the car park.

Parking Lat/Long: 50.611299, -2.130196
Parking Postcode: BH20 5PF
Kimmeridge Bay OS map co-ordinate: SY 907 791

Map: OS Explorer Map OL15 (1:25 000) Purbeck and South Dorset

Accessibility

It's just a couple of minutes walk from the car park down to the main part of the bay. Take care walking around, especially getting to Broad Bench and the Eastern Ledges as you will have to walk over uneven rocks which are not always stable. The rocks and the ledges can also get slippery, especially the central ledge in the main bay, so exercise great caution when walking on these surfaces and always wear sturdy walking boots. There is no disabled access to the main part of the bay but it is possible to shoot from the car park.

There is a toilet block in the small car park (reserved for vehicles towing boats) which is to be found on the east of the main car park. Kimmeridge is at its most photogenic at a mid to low tide so check tide tables when planning a visit. From a safety point of view it's also vital to know what the tide is doing – it's possible to get cut off at Broad Bench and the western ledges. There is a visitor centre on the east side of the bay by the fishermen's huts and it's possible to drive down to the boat park here. This is useful access for the disabled, but there is a set of gates here which are locked at dusk so remember to move your car before then.

The cliffs at Kimmeridge are highly unstable and there are frequent land slips. Do not stand at the base of the cliffs.

Kimmeridge Bay is private land – part of the Smedmore Estate – a charge is made for parking to help maintain the car park and toilets. In contrast to nearby Durdle Door there are no restrictions on commercial photography.

Best Time of Year/Day

Autumn and winter from afternoon until sunset are the best times to shoot Clavell's Tower and the main section of the bay. Clavell's Pier is best shot at sunset from early autumn until spring and shooting from the eastern ledges works well at sunset in summer.

There is a sad atmosphere in the ghost village of Tyneham. In late 1943 the village and 7,500 acres of land surrounding it were commandeered by the War Office for use as firing ranges for training troops prior to the D-Day landings.

Two hundred and twenty five people were relocated and the last one to leave the village left a note on the church door which said: "Please treat the church and houses with care; we have given up our homes where many of us lived for generations to help win the war to keep men free. We shall return one day and thank you for treating the village kindly." The measure was supposed to be temporary but the land was never returned.

The village is now open to visitors at weekends and during holidays. Most of the buildings are derelict but the old schoolhouse and the church are preserved as museums. One benefit of the MOD's ownership of the land is that there has been no development and despite the shelling the area has become a haven for wildlife.

What to Shoot and Viewpoints

Tyneham is not an easy place to photograph and because of the access restrictions is difficult to shoot in ideal light. It is however worth a visit – perhaps as part of a shoot at Worbarrow Bay – even if you decide not to take any shots.

Viewpoint 1 – St Mary's Church

The church dates back to the thirteenth century and photographs well from the churchyard with the Purbeck hills behind it. Interior shots are also possible though space is limited and, because of other visitors, your best option might be to hand-hold using a high ISO.

Viewpoint 2 – The School House

The school house is well-preserved and, like the church, both exterior and interior shots are possible. For the interior hand-holding using high ISO is probably the most practical approach. Look also for detail shots such as the name tags on the coat hooks.

Viewpoint 3 – The Phone Box

There is a K1 Mark 236 phone box in the village. It is not the original which was destroyed in 1985 when Tyneham was being used as film location, but a replacement bought by the film company.

Viewpoint 4 – Derelict Cottages

There are a number of derelict cottages around the village, some of which can be photographed across a pond and surrounded by overgrown foliage. For something more atmospheric, you could try black and white or infrared shots of these subjects.

Left: The K1 Mk 236 phone box in Tyneham village.
Fuji X-Pro2, 10-24mm f/4 at 15mm, ISO 400, 1/130 second at f/8

How To Get Here

Tyneham is situated about 3.5 miles south of Wareham and 10 miles west of Swanage. Just outside Corfe Castle on the A351 turn into Tyneham Road (the turning opposite the National Trust Visitor Centre and the Studland Road). After about a mile and a half you pass through the village of Church Knowle. Continue on the Tyneham Road past the turnings for Kimmeridge and Steeple. You will then go up a steep hill with a hairpin bend at the top. Do not follow the bend of the road round to the right, but bear left (signposted to Tyneham). This road takes you through the army ranges so is only open when there is no firing taking place. A few hundred yards down the road there is a turning on the left which takes you down to the car park at Tyneham.

Parking Lat/Long: 50.621156, -2.169613
Parking Postcode: BH20 5DE
Worbarrow Bay OS map co-ordinate: SY 880 801

Map: OS Explorer Map OL15 (1:25 000) Purbeck and South Dorset

Accessibility

The car park at Tyneham is run by the MOD; there are no ticket machines or parking attendants but there is an honesty box with a suggested parking fee. Proceeds go towards maintaining the village. There is a gate at the top of the road which is only open at weekends and during holidays. It is locked at dusk. There are toilets near the car park. Disabled access is possible but not to all of the buildings in the village. See notes on army range restrictions on p.81.

Best Time of Year/Day

Being on the army ranges the village is only accessible at weekends and holidays. The gates at the top of the road down to Tyneham are locked from dusk until around 9.00am, so shooting in early or late light is difficult. A bright overcast day works well.

Opposite: Rows of desks in the school house.
Fuji X-Pro2, 10-24mm at 10mm, ISO6400, 1/20 second at f/5.6

Worbarrow Bay is another of the less-visited parts of the Purbeck coast, being on MOD land it is only accessible when the Lulworth Ranges are open. It is accessed from the deserted village of Tyneham (page 76) and it makes sense to visit the two locations on the same trip. At the eastern end of the bay is a distinctively-shaped promontory known as Worbarrow Tout – 'tout' being old English for 'look-out'.

The bay has a shingle beach sloping down to the sea like Durdle Door and Chesil Bank. The surrounding cliffs are sandstone, which glows attractively in the evening light. The bay curves gently around giving a natural flow to shots along the shoreline, either towards the Tout in the east or Mupe Rocks in the west.

What to Shoot and Viewpoints

Park at Tyneham and follow the level footpath for just over a kilometre until you reach the bay. You enter the bay by the Tout; you can shoot from here, in the middle of the bay or further to the west by 'Cow Corner'. At the west end of the bay is the hill fort of Flower's Barrow which gives an elevated view across the bay.

Looking towards Worbarrow Tout from Flower's Barrow on a summer evening. Pentax 67II, 45mm f/4, Fuji Velvia 50

Viewpoint 1 – From the base of Worbarrow Tout

On the left of the bay at the base of the Tout there is a scattering of rugged rocks. Seek out an interesting arrangement to frame the view for a shot looking over to the far side of the bay and Mupe Rocks.

Viewpoint 2 – Worbarrow Tout from the Shore

This is a viewpoint that works well with the sun low in the sky, casting warm light onto the Tout. Walk towards the western end of the bay. You'll probably want to set up roughly in the middle of the bay to exploit the curve of the shoreline. This is approximate so use your own judgement. At lower tides there will be rocks revealed. Many of these are white in colour, with interesting shapes and texture. Using an ND filter to extend exposure times and shooting the waves as they rush back towards the sea can create interesting patterns as the waves wash between them.

Viewpoint 3 – Towards Mupe Rocks

This is a composition that works well anywhere between the middle of the bay and the western end – spend some time seeking out a strong foreground. On a high tide you can use the curve of the bay to lead the eye through the shot and when it is lower, look out for some of the many bumpy rocks embedded in the shingle.

Viewpoint 4 – From Flower's Barrow

To reach Flower's Barrow from the bay, walk up to the cliff top from where you first enter the bay. It's a steep climb however and an alternative is to park in the car park at Whiteway Hill between Tyneham and Lulworth and then walk along the footpath through the army ranges for just under 2 kilometres. There are great views across Worbarrow Bay to the Tout, but also to the west over Arish Mell towards Mupe Bay.

Winter sunset, looking towards Mupe Rocks. Canon 1Ds Mk II, 24-105mm at 60mm, ISO 100, 25 seconds at f/22

Towards the Tout from the middle of the bay.
Pentax 67II, 55mm, Fuji Velvia 50

How To Get Here

Worbarrow Bay is 3.5 miles south west of Wareham. Just outside Corfe Castle on the A351 turn into Tyneham Road – the turning opposite the National Trust Visitor Centre and the Studland Road. After about a mile and a half you pass through the village of Church Knowle. Continue on the Tyneham Road past the turnings for Kimmeridge and Steeple. You will then go up a steep hill with a hairpin bend at the top. Do not follow the bend of the road round to the right but bear left (signposted to Tyneham). This road takes you through the army ranges so is only open when there is no firing taking place. A few hundred yards down the road there is a turning on the left which takes you down to the car park at Tyneham. To get to the car park at Whiteway Hill continue on the Tyneham Road for a few hundred yards more and you will see it on the left.

Parking Lat/Long: 50.621588, -2.1681798
Parking Postcode: BH20 QN
Parking OS map co-ordinate: SY 881 802

Map: OS Explorer Map OL15 (1:25 000) Purbeck and South Dorset

Accessibility

The car park at Tyneham is run by the MOD; there are no ticket machines or parking attendants but there is an honesty box with a suggested parking fee. Proceeds go towards maintaining Tyneham village. There is a gate at the top of the road which is only open at weekends and during holidays. It is locked at dusk so if shooting the sunset, allow yourself enough time to get back to your car and get out of the car park. See notes on army range restrictions on p.81.

The walk to Worbarrow Bay is level and easy underfoot. Disabled access to the beach itself is not possible. There are toilets near the car park.

Best Time of Year/Day

The gates at the top of the road down to Tyneham are locked overnight and not opened until around 9.00am, meaning sunrise shoots from the beach are not really possible. From early November through till mid-February the sun sets over the sea and shots from the beach work well. If shooting from Flower's Barrow, sunsets at this time of year will provide attractive side lighting into the bay and on the Tout. In mid-winter the sun rises slightly to the left of the Tout as viewed from Flower's Barrow, so you have a good chance of getting some sunrise colour from this viewpoint.

Mupe Bay to Bat's Head

The section of coast between Mupe Bay in the east and Bat's Head in the west includes Durdle Door and Lulworth Cove, the most visited locations on the Dorset coast. The map below details the locations and viewpoints along this stretch that are featured in this book. It serves also as a reminder that this book is a starting point for further exploration. Use an OS map and follow the coastal footpaths to other and perhaps equally good photo locations, as Thomas Hardy would say; 'far from the madding crowd.'

The 'classic' view of Durdle Door from the beach with the warm glow of the evening sun and a rainbow to set it off.
Canon 5D Mk III, 16-35mm at 21mm, ISO 125, 2.5 seconds at f/11

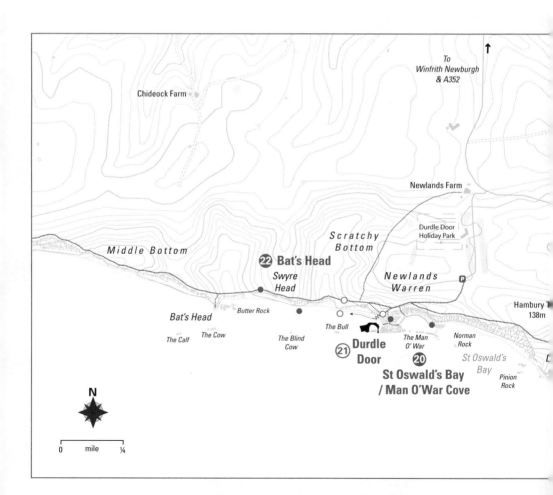

Lulworth Army Range Restrictions

Just west of Kimmeridge Bay the village of Tyneham, Worbarrow Bay, Mupe Bay and the eastern end of Lulworth Cove all lie within Lulworth Army Ranges used by the Armoured Fighting Vehicles Gunnery School for shooting practice.

There is no access to these areas from Monday to Friday and certain weekends.

When Open

Lulworth Range walks are normally accessible every Saturday and Sunday except for six weekends in the year. They are also open during Christmas, Easter, all of August and all Public Holidays. Access information can be gained by contacting the Range.

A recording of up to date information can be heard on **01929 462721 Ext. 4819** or visit: *www.gov.uk/government/publications/lulworth-firing-notice*

There is no access if red flags are flown or lamps lit.

Over 70,000 high explosive shells are fired each year. These are cleared but please follow the following safety rules.

- Do not pick up any ordnance (shells, cartridges etc.).
- Do not enter the Ranges if the gate is locked.
- Do not stray from the path which is clearly marked by plain wooden posts with yellow bands.
- Do not allow children or dogs to stray.
- Do not touch or pick up any metal objects lying on the ground.
- Please keep away from all buildings, except for Tyneham Church, the School House and toilet facilities.

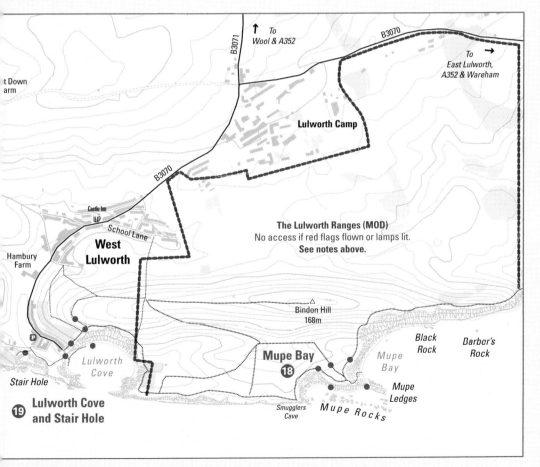

Mupe Ledges. Spring sunrise. The sun is rising over the land, but this provides attractive side lighting on the ledges. A mid-tide means the waves are washing up between the ledges. Nikon D800, 16-35mm at 16mm, ISO 100, 5 seconds at f/16

Mupe Bay is almost a mirror image of the neighbouring Worbarrow Bay, they are divided by Arish Mell, a small embayment and beach. Located within the army ranges Mupe Bay is only accessible during holidays and at weekends – this gives it a wonderfully isolated atmosphere. The rugged nature of the coastline with its jagged ledges and sea stacks enhance this wild feel.

It's a bit of a trek and there is a steep climb at the start of the walk to Mupe Bay. This approach combined with the access restrictions means that you'll often have the place to yourself.

What to Shoot and Viewpoints

From School Lane take the footpath up the hill. It's a steep climb but once at the top the rest of the walk is easy. Take the footpath to the left onto the army ranges and follow it across Bindon Hill for about 1.5 kilometres. You will see steps down to the western end of the bay and Mupe Ledges. From here there are shots along the ledges or across to Mupe Rocks or you can walk further around the bay and shoot towards Worbarrow. From the cliff top there are shots along the coastline in both directions and over to Mupe Rocks.

Viewpoint 1 – Mupe Rocks

Mupe Rocks look menacing – the larger sea stack in the middle of the group really draws the eye. They make a great minimalist study in their own right, especially with waves washing around them during long exposures or as a background focal point when shooting across the ledges. With a higher tide you're probably best taking the more minimalist approach, but with a lower tide, it's difficult to resist putting the rocky ledges in the foreground.

Viewpoint 2 – Mupe Ledges

With a mid to low tide the ledges are nicely exposed and make dramatic leading lines through compositions. With a mid-level tide waves wash up in the channels between the ledges, helping to define and separate them. You can find viewpoints on the ledges either to include Mupe Rocks in the frame or not.

Viewpoint 3 – From the Cliff Top

From the cliff top there are far-reaching views both east and west but one of the best spots to set up is on a small corner just above the ledges. From here you can shoot to the south east encompassing the ledges, the sea stacks and views towards Arish Mell and Worbarrow Tout.

How To Get Here

Mupe Bay parking is at West Lulworth, as for Lulworth Cove. The bay is just under a mile east of Lulworth Cove and 7.5 miles south west of Wareham. From Wareham take the A352 towards Dorchester. After a mile and a half take the first turning on the left, the B3070 towards East Lulworth. After approximately 4 miles you will pass through East Lulworth with the Weld Arms pub on your left. The road bends round to the right and you will see Lulworth Castle on your right. Keep going to the end of the road and turn left at the T-junction towards West Lulworth. Drive through the village with the church on your right and various B & B's on your left. At the end of the road there is a large pay and display car park. While it's not cheap, the tickets are also valid for the car park at nearby Durdle Door.

Once you've parked your car turn left out of the car park and walk back through the village. Take the second turning on the right, School Lane, opposite the Castle Inn. The footpath up to Bindon Hill is about 150m along the road on the right.

Parking Lat/Long: 50.620135, -2.254451
Parking Postcode: BH20 5RS
Mupe Bay OS map co-ordinate: SY 839 797

Map: OS Explorer Map OL15 (1:25 000) Purbeck and South Dorset

Accessibility

This is not a long walk but is quite strenuous and steep at the beginning. Once you've got to the top it is a gentle walk down to Mupe Bay. There is no disabled access. It used to be possible to get up to Bindon Hill following a footpath from the beach but, due to coastal erosion, this route is no longer possible. There is a route from the far side of the Cove, but this is not really any easier.

There are toilets in the visitor centre near the car park as well as on the road down to the beach. There is a café and fish and chip shop by the car park as well as various pubs and eateries in the village.

See notes on army range restrictions on p.81.

Best Time of Year/Day

Mupe Bay is best photographed in the winter months due to the angle of sunrise and sunset. Although sunrise is probably the most popular option it also looks good towards the end of the day as the side lighting can reveal the texture of the ledges and help to give depth to the scene.

Opposite: Mupe Rocks on a stormy morning at high tide.
Canon 5D Mk II, 17-40mm f/4 at 17mm, ISO 200, 13 seconds at f/11

Anyone who has studied geography at school will be familiar with Lulworth Cove. The horseshoe-shaped cove was formed by coastal erosion and sits next door to that other geological wonder, Durdle Door. This location receives around 500,000 visitors annually, an incredible number for such a small place.

This may seem discouraging for some photographers who prefer their landscapes to be devoid of all evidence of human life. But don't let this statistic put you off, the majority of tourists visit Lulworth in July and August so, if you go out of season and at the right time of day, you can create people-free shots.

And there's a lot to shoot here; views of the cove from the hills high up above the cove, shoreline shots across limestone ridges and views across Stair Hole, a Lulworth Cove in the making.

What to Shoot and Viewpoints

From the car park it's a short stroll down the road to the beach, or a short but steep climb up the hill on the south west corner of the car park to reach the cliffs above Stair Hole (VP 3). To get to Viewpoint 4 follow the directions for Mupe Bay (see page 84) but once up the slope at the beginning of the walk carry straight on along the footpath rather than turning left onto the range walks.

Viewpoint 1 – From the Western Side of the Cove

From the car park walk down the road towards the beach. Just before you get to the beach take the footpath on the right up to the small cliff above the bay. From here there are wide angle shots following the curve of the shore round to the eastern flank of the bay.

Viewpoint 2 – From the Shore

There are a number of features along the shoreline which make useful foreground interest: pebbles, boulders and limestone ridges. With a wide angle lens there are powerful compositions sweeping along the shoreline towards the eastern flank of the cove. These compositions work well with exposures of a couple of seconds or so, capturing the backwash of waves. Alternatively, from the middle of the cove you can shoot out towards its entrance, including both headlands, creating an implied triangle with the two sides of the cove and a foreground object such as a boulder.

Viewpoint 3 – Looking across Stair Hole.

From the cliffs above Stair Hole you can shoot eastwards towards the cove. As well as having waves crashing into Stair Hole in the foreground, this viewpoint also highlights the folded limestone strata know as the 'Lulworth Crumple.'

Viewpoint 4 – From the Cliffs next to Bindon Hill

It's a steep climb to get to this viewpoint but it's worth the effort as you get a panoramic view of the bay revealing its unique shape and giving a useful overview of the location. This is the best place to shoot from to reveal the true character of this location.

Winter sunrise looking across Stair Hole towards Lulworth Cove.
Fuji X-E1, 10-24mm f/4 at 14.5mm, ISO 100, 10 seconds at f/11

How To Get Here

Lulworth Cove is 7 miles south west of Wareham. From Wareham take the A352 towards Dorchester. After just under a mile and a half take the first turning on the left, the B3070 towards East Lulworth. After approximately 4 miles you will pass through East Lulworth with the Weld Arms pub on your left. The road bends round to the right and you will see Lulworth Castle on your right. Keep going to the end of the road and turn left at the T-junction towards West Lulworth. Drive through the village, with the church on your right and various B & B's on your left. At the end of the road there is a large pay and display car park. While it's not cheap, the tickets are also valid for the car park at nearby Durdle Door.

Parking Lat/Long: 50.620135, -2.254451
Parking Postcode: BH20 5RS
Lulworth Cove OS map co-ordinate: SY 824 799

Map: OS Explorer Map OL15 (1:25 000) Purbeck and South Dorset

Accessibility

The shoreline views and views from the west side of the cove are short, gentle walks from the car park. The viewpoint from Stair Hole is a short but steep walk and care must be taken, especially when descending, as it can get slippery. It is a steep climb to the cliff top views next to Bindon Hill. Disabled access is possible to the beach but not the other viewpoints.

There are toilets in the visitor centre near the car park as well as on the road down to the beach. There is a café and fish and chip shop by the car park as well as various pubs and eateries in the village.

Lulworth Cove is privately owned by the Lulworth Estate who impose restrictions on commercial photography on their land. If you intend to sell your images contact them to obtain permission.

See notes on army range restrictions on p.81.

Best Time of Year/Day

Viewpoint 1 looks its best at sunrise between October and March. Shots from the shore work best in afternoon and evening from mid-December until mid-March when the late afternoon sun casts a warm glow over the cliffs on the far side of the cove. Shooting across Stair Hole towards the Cove is a sunrise composition which works best from mid-September to mid-March. Shooting from Viewpoint 4 is best done at sunset from the end of September until the beginning of March.

Opposite top: Late afternoon sun lights up the eastern flank of the cove at the beginning of March. Canon 5D Mk III, 16-35mm f/2.8 at 16mm, ISO 100, 2 seconds at f/14.

Above: View from the western side of the cove at sunrise. Pentax 67II, 55mm f/4, Fuji Velvia 50

If St Oswald's Bay – also known locally as Man O' War Bay – was situated anywhere else on the Dorset coast, it would be one of the must-visit locations for photographers. With the beautiful half-moon shaped Man O' War Cove on its western end, rocky ledges in the foreground, rock stacks in the middle distance and rugged headlands in the background, it is extremely photogenic.

Sitting right next door to Durdle Door means it gets far less attention than it should. This is a good thing as it means that even in summer it gets far less crowded than its neighbour.

What to Shoot and Viewpoints

From the car park at Durdle Door follow the footpath down to the cliffs above the shore. You have views of both St Oswald's Bay and Durdle Door from here. You can then follow the footpath down to St Oswald's Bay.

Viewpoint 1 – Cliff Top Views

From the cliffs it is possible to shoot across the whole of the bay, with Man O' War Cove prominent immediately below. The cliff edge is fenced off for safety reasons (there have been several quite severe landslips along this stretch of coastline in recent years) but good shots are possible from inside the fence. Some people have been known to climb over the fence to obtain a better viewpoint, but this is not recommended.

Post sunset colour above St Oswald's Bay at the end of January. Canon 5D Mk III, 16-35mm at 29mm, ISO 100, 30 secs at f/11

Viewpoint 2 – From the Western End of the Bay

Immediately in front of the steps down to the bay are some interesting fins of rock which stretch out into the sea and work well as lead-in lines. As there are high cliffs both right and left contrast can be a real problem depending on the light. The shape of the cliffs makes the use of graduated filters tricky so you may find it best to bracket exposures and blend in processing to capture the full range of tones in the the scene (see page 238).

Viewpoint 3 – Across the Ledges to Dungy Head

If you walk around to the far side of the cove you will see some rocky ledges pointing towards the headland of Dungy Head. It is possible to include these in the foreground pointing towards Dungy Head and also include the rock stack in the middle of the bay. A longish exposure of between 10 and 30 seconds works well, with the waves washing over the foreground ledges.

How To Get Here

Man O' War Bay is 9.5 miles south east of Dorchester and 8.5 miles south west of Wareham. From Wareham take the A352 towards Dorchester. After a mile and a half take the first turning on the left, the B3070 towards East Lulworth. After approx. 4 miles you pass through East Lulworth with the Weld Arms pub on your left. The road bends to the right and you will see Lulworth Castle on your right. Keep going to the end of the road and turn left at the T-junction towards West Lulworth. Go through the village and turn right into Church Road just past the church. At the top of the hill, turn left towards Durdle Door Holiday Park. Drive through the holiday park to get to the car park. Parking charges are not cheap but tickets are also valid for Lulworth Cove.

From October to March the holiday park is open from 8 a.m. to 4 p.m. Outside these hours you will need to park some way down Church Road, before the double yellow lines and then walk. It may be possible to park off the road near the entrance to Newlands Farm, 200m beyond the turning for the holiday park.

Parking Lat/Long: 50.624067, -2.269125
Parking Postcode: BH20 5PU
OS map co-ordinate: SY 811 804

Map: OS Explorer Map OL15 (1:25 000) Purbeck and South Dorset

Accessibility

Access down to St Oswald's Bay is via a steep footpath. It is chalky, with loose stones on top and easy to slip on, so appropriate footwear is essential. The steps down from the cliff are also steep and can be slippery in winter. A reasonable level of fitness is essential for the climb back up and disabled access is not possible. There are toilets on the holiday park, as well as a bar and a shop.

Best Time of Year/Day

St Oswald's Bay really comes into its own on a winter sunrise when you can shoot towards the rising sun and any colour in the sky; this is a fairly limited window from mid-November until early February. Shots are possible during the day all year round but because of the cliffs you lose the light quite early. One possibility in spring and early autumn is to shoot in St Oswald's Bay in the afternoon and then move next door to Durdle Door once you lose the light.

Opposite: Winter sunrise from the eastern end of Man O' War Cove. Canon 5D Mk II, 17-40mm at 17mm, ISO 100, 2 exposures blended

Lulworth Cove. Late September sunset from the cliff top.
Canon 5D Mk III, 16-35mm f/2.8 at 22mm, ISO 100, 8 seconds at f/16

Durdle Door probably shares the honours with Lulworth Cove as being the location in Dorset which most people remember from geography lessons at school. The limestone arch is a striking sight whether viewed from the clifftop path or the shore. The name Durdle comes from the Old English 'thirl', meaning to bore or drill.

Unlike nearby Lulworth Cove, which appears in Far From the Madding Crowd as 'Lulwind Cove,' Durdle Door is not a location featured in any of Thomas Hardy's novels; it has however been used as a location in both film versions of Far From the Madding Crowd as well as various other films and music videos.

What to Shoot and Viewpoints

Follow the footpath down from the car park until you reach the cliff top above Durdle Door. You can take the coast path to your right, or continue down the steps to the beach.

Viewpoint 1 – From the Coast Path

There are several spots along the coast path where you can shoot east, back towards Durdle Door. From the top of the first small hill it is possible to get a wide angle shot along the path which also includes St Oswald's Bay in the composition. The grasses on the cliff edge can also be used to good effect, especially when low evening sun brings out their texture.

Viewpoint 2 – Looking West from the Clifftop

From the top of the steps leading down to the beach a wide angle composition encompasses Durdle Door on the left and the cliffs on the right, leading towards Bat's Head (a smaller version of Durdle Door). The wider you can go with this shot the better. There are also interesting angles from about half way down the steps.

Viewpoint 3 – From the Shore

Walk along the shore for a couple of hundred metres and you can compose a shot following the curve of the shoreline back to the rock arch. Be careful not to walk too far as the perspective from further along makes the arch 'close up'. The shingle beach slopes down to the sea and the waves washing up over the bank can be shot with exposures of 1–2 seconds to create some foreground interest. With shutter speeds longer than this the waves start to lose their texture and, as a general rule, the backwash of the waves will create more interesting patterns than breaking waves do.

Viewpoint 4 – Sunrise and Set Through the Arch

For a couple of weeks around the winter solstice the sun rises and sets in such a position that it can be shot through the arch of Durdle Door. Use an app such as the Photographer's Ephemeris to help you identify the best time of year and the best position on the beach for this shot. Setting a small aperture such as f/16 or f/22 can result in a diffraction 'sunstar'. If you can time the shot so that there is a wave pulling back to sea in the foreground, so much the better, and it helps if there is some cloud in the sky. In order to get all the elements coming together in one shot you may find that repeated visits (possibly over a period of years rather than just a few days!) are necessary.

How To Get Here

Durdle Door Bay is 9.5 miles south east of Dorchester and 8.5 miles south west of Wareham. From Wareham take the A352 towards Dorchester. After just under a mile and a half take the first turning on the left, the B3070 towards East Lulworth. After approximately 4 miles you will pass through East Lulworth with the Weld Arms pub on your left. The road bends round to the right and you will see Lulworth Castle on your right. Keep going to the end of the road and turn left at the T-junction towards West Lulworth. Drive through the village and turn right into Church Road just past the church. At the top of the hill turn left towards Durdle Door holiday park. Drive through the holiday park to get to the car park. The parking charges are not insignificant but tickets are also valid for the car park at Lulworth Cove.

From October to March the holiday park is open from 8 a.m. to 4 p.m. Outside these hours you will need to park some way down Church Road, before the double yellow lines and then walk. It may be possible to park off the road near the entrance to Newlands Farm, 200m beyond the turning for the holiday park.

Parking Lat/Long: 50.624067, -2.269125
Parking Postcode: BH20 5PU
Durdle Door OS map co-ordinate: SY 804 802

Map: OS Explorer Map OL15 (1:25 000) Purbeck and South Dorset

Accessibility

Getting down to Durdle Door is by a steep footpath. The path is chalky with loose stones on top and easy to slip on so appropriate footwear is advised. The steps down from the cliff are also steep and can be slippery in winter. A reasonable level of fitness is essential for the climb back up and disabled access is not possible. There are toilets on the holiday park as well as a bar and a shop.

Best Time of Year/Day

In mid- April and mid-September the sun sets in such a position that it lights the face of Durdle Door, creating a warm glow. Slightly earlier and later than these times, the edge of the rock arch is lit by the setting sun. From mid-December through till mid-January it is possible to shoot the rising and setting sun through the arch. Sunsets from the cliff top (Viewpoint 2) work well from September through till the end of March.

Although spring and early autumn are the favourite times for shots from the shore and the coast path, this was taken at the end of January with the late afternoon sun casting attractive side lighting over the foreground.
Canon 5D Mk III, 16-35mm f/2.8 at 18mm, ISO 100, 1/30 second at f/11

The sun rising through the arch in mid-winter.
Canon 5D Mk III, Zeiss 21mm f/2.8, ISO 100, 6 seconds at f/22

About a kilometre west of Durdle Door is a small chalk headland known as Bat's Head. There is a small natural arch in the headland – a kind of mini Durdle Door – known as Bat's Hole. It is less remarkable than Durdle Door but there are some great shots to be had if you point your camera in the opposite direction, and it makes a change from photographing its more iconic neighbour.

What to Shoot and Viewpoints

You can park at Durdle Door (see page 92) and shoot from the coast path or walk along the beach from Durdle Door for a shoreline view. If you don't fancy the steep climb on the coast path, there is an easier route to Swyre Head (see How to Get Here, below)

Viewpoint 1 – From the Shore

Follow the footpath from the car park down to the cliff above Durdle Door, then the steps down to the beach. You will see Bat's Head to the west. You have the option of shooting with a long lens from Durdle Door or walking along the beach for a closer view – though make sure

you know what the tide is doing as high tide gets very close to the base of the cliff in places. There is a chalk stack near Bat's Head which can be included in a shot of the headland or makes an interesting study in its own right.

Viewpoint 2 – From the Clifftop

If you walk west along the coast path from Durdle Door for about three-quarters of a kilometre you will reach Swyre Head (not to be confused with the other Swyre Head further east between Chapman's Pool and Kimmeridge). From here you can shoot down towards Bat's Head and the nearby sea stack. In late spring and summer, you may find wildflowers which you can include in the foreground.

Opposite: VP2. Sunset from Swyre Head at the end of June, showing the natural arch of Bat's Head in the distance. Canon 1Ds Mk II, 17-40mm f/4 at 17mm, ISO 100, 0.4 second at f/16

Left: VP1. Looking along the shoreline towards Bat's Head at sunset in September. Fuji X-Pro2, 10-24mm f/4 at 19mm, ISO 200, 30 seconds at f/16, LEE 6-stop ND & 0.9 medium grad

How To Get Here

Bat's Head is around a kilometre west of Durdle Door and you can use the same car park (see page 92). Alternatively for a slightly easier walk to the cliff-top viewpoint, park as close as you can to the entrance to Durdle Door holiday park – you may find parking on the verge just past it or further down Church Road. Walk through the entrance to the holiday park and immediately fork right, rather than going down the hill. Walk past some converted farm buildings to a footpath on your left, signposted towards Ringstead. Follow this footpath for a couple of hundred metres to a gate on your left. There is a footpath through a field which takes you through the wonderfully-named Scratchy Bottom to the coast path. Walk west towards Swyre Head and Bat's Head.

Parking Lat/Long: 50.624067, -2.269125
Parking Postcode: BH20 5PU
Bat's Head OS map co-ordinate: SY 795 803

Map: OS Explorer Map OL15 (1:25 000) Purbeck and South Dorset

Accessibility

If you follow the coast path from Durdle Door there is a very steep climb. Getting down to the beach at Durdle Door is via a steep, chalky path and a set of steep steps which can be slippery, so make sure you wear good walking boots. The footpath through Scratchy Bottom takes you through fields which may have cattle grazing in them. There is no disabled access.

Best Time of Year/Day

Early morning shots work from November until February. Sunsets are best from mid-September to April. Shots are possible at other times, but the sun will be setting over the land, so you may find you are not shooting towards the most intense colour.

East Dorset – Introduction

With its urban sprawl of Poole, Bournemouth and Christchurch, a conurbation which stretches for some 15 miles along the coast, east Dorset has a completely different character to the rest of the county. Until 1974, when the Local Government Act came into force, Bournemouth and Christchurch were not part of Dorset and there are those, even today, who do not consider them to be 'proper' Dorset. The 1974 reorganisation of the county boundaries led to a substantial increase in the county's population and the south east conurbation is now home to around half of it.

The area is more built-up and with far more industry than the rest of the county, most of this being recent development. Just 200 years ago the area between Poole and Christchurch was open heathland. Today Bournemouth has a population of around 190,000 and the total population of the conurbation is almost half a million.

All of this may make the area sound unattractive for photography and while it's true that most photographers probably head straight for nearby Purbeck, they'd be missing a trick if they didn't spend some time in east Dorset. There are some beautiful areas in between the housing estates and shopping centres: the historic centre of Christchurch with its Priory Church and pretty river frontage, the remaining heathland at Hengistbury Head, the famously expensive beach chalets on Mudeford Spit and Stanpit Marsh Nature Reserve, to name but a few. Just escaping the urban sprawl to the north is the quaint market town of Wimborne Minster and the surrounding villages and countryside.

A mirror-like reflection of a boat at low tide in Poole Harbour. Late January sunset. Canon 5D, 17-40mm f/4L at 27mm, ISO 100, 15 seconds at f/16, LEE 0.6 soft grad

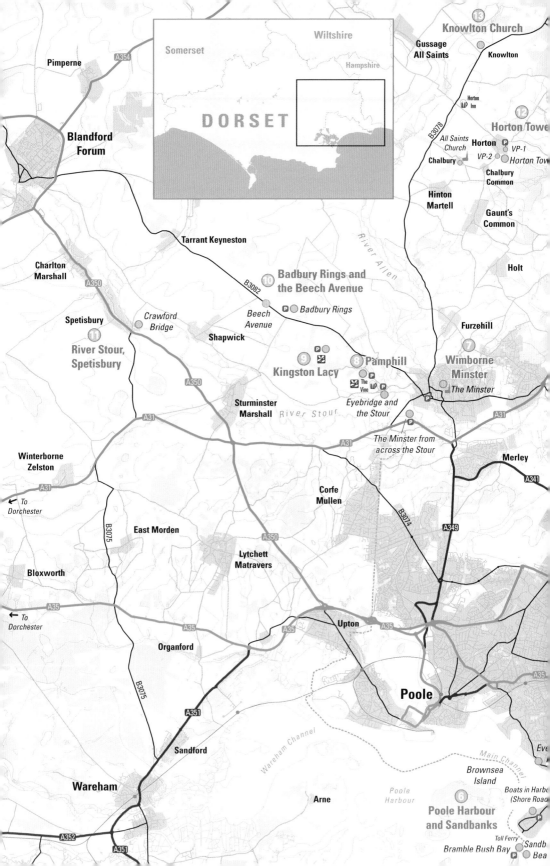

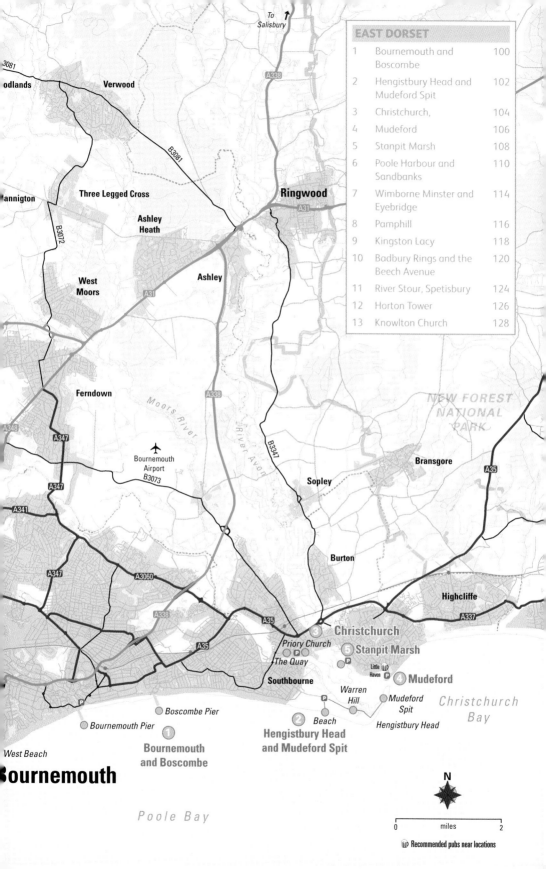

To
Salisbury

3081

odlands

Verwood

annington

Three Legged Cross

Ringwood

Ashley Heath

West Moors

Ashley

Ferndown

Moors River

River Avon

NEW FOREST NATIONAL PARK

Bournemouth Airport

Sopley

Bransgore

Burton

Highcliffe

Christchurch

Priory Church

Stanpit Marsh

The Quay

Little Haven

Mudeford

Southbourne

Warren Hill

Mudeford Spit

Christchurch Bay

Boscombe Pier

Beach

Hengistbury Head

Bournemouth Pier

Bournemouth and Boscombe

Hengistbury Head and Mudeford Spit

West Beach

Bournemouth

Poole Bay

N

0   miles   2

Recommended pubs near locations

It's probably not unreasonable to suggest that Bournemouth itself counts among the less photogenic places in Dorset. Traditionally regarded as a rather sleepy retirement town, modern Bournemouth is in fact much livelier than its reputation – a popular destination for stag and hen weekends, and home to numerous pubs, clubs and pole-dancing clubs.

All is not lost for photographers however. The town is rightly proud of the ten miles of golden beach which run from Hengistbury Head to Sandbanks. It is probably best to concentrate photographic efforts around these beaches and the cliff tops, where there are great views both to the west and to Purbeck in the east. The two piers – one at Bournemouth, the other at Boscombe – make good focal points for cliff-top views along the beach and are also good subjects in their own right. Other possibilities include rows of beach huts, breakwaters with waves washing around them and the occasional fishing boat tied up on the beach.

What To Shoot and Viewpoints

Viewpoint 1 – West Beach

Park at the Branksome Chine car park and walk onto the beach or promenade. There are views here both to the east, towards the pier and west, towards Poole and Purbeck. For foreground interest there are stone breakwaters or, further east, wooden groynes. Along the stretch of beach near Durley Chine and Alum Chine there are sometimes fishing boats tied up.

Viewpoint 2 – Bournemouth Pier

From the Bath Road car park walk down the steps to the beach. The pier is probably best shot early or late in the day when there are fewer people around. This works well photographed from either the east or the west depending on the time of day and whether you want to shoot towards any sunrise/sunset colour or prefer to have warm light falling onto the pier itself. In terms of compositions it's probably best to keep things simple; use the waves or shoreline to create lead-in lines and foreground interest.

Like anywhere, unusual or extreme weather including squalls, strong winds, high tides, big waves, rain showers, rainbows or snow will all help to make a more dramatic and unusual composition.

Viewpoint 3 – Boscombe Pier

There is plenty of pay and display parking near the pier, in Sea Road and Undercliff Drive. From these car parks it's only a short walk to the pier.

Boscombe Pier was built at the end of the 19th century and renovated in the post-war years and then again in the noughties. The entrance building is modernist 1950s style and is Grade II listed. The renovated pier features a central windbreak which lends itself to some interesting compositions. The classic shot is a symmetrical composition with the windbreak in the centre of the frame, but other placements of this feature are certainly possible.

Like nearby Bournemouth Pier shooting from the beach, either east or west, can give some very pleasing compositions with options for both ends of the day.

Boats tied up on the beach at Durley Chine.
Pentax 67II, 45mm f/4.0, Fuji Velvia 50, f/16

There are excellent views towards Purbeck from the western side of Bournemouth beach. Pentax 67II, 45mm f/4.0, Fuji Velvia 50, f/16

Somewhat rare snow on the beach in front of Bournemouth Pier.
Canon 5D Mk II, 17-40mm f/4L at 23mm, ISO 100, 6 seconds at f/22, LEE 1.2 ND & 0.6 soft grad, polariser.

How To Get Here

Bournemouth is located on the south coast, 25 miles south west of Southampton. From the east drive west on the A31. Take the first exit at the Ashley Heath roundabout onto the A338 into Bournemouth.

For the **Branksome Chine** car park stay on the A338 until you reach the County Gates Gyratory known locally as the Frizzell roundabout, as the insurance company's headquarters (now Liverpool Victoria) are in the centre of it, and take the second exit onto The Avenue (B3065). The car park is at the bottom of the hill where the road bends sharply to the right.

For the **Bath Road** car park turn left onto the A338 at Ashley Heath and stay on the A338 past the turning for Bournemouth Hospital. At the next roundabout, with Asda on your left, take the first exit onto St Paul's Road (A35) and then at the next roundabout, the third exit onto Holdenhurst Road (B3066). Cross two further roundabouts, staying on the B3066. The Bath Road car park is on your left.

To get to **Boscombe Pier**, continue on the A338 past the turning for the hospital then take the slip road towards Littledown and Boscombe. Take the third exit on the roundabout onto Holdenhurst Road and turn left onto Ashley Road. After half a mile, turn right into Shelley Road and left at the end into Palmerston Road. Stay on Palmerston Road for about half a mile then turn left into St John's Road. At the end of the road, turn right into Sea Road and follow this to the car park.

Branksome Chine Parking Lat/Long: 50.706870, -1.909070
Parking Postcode: BH13 6LP
OS Map grid ref: SZ 065 896

Bath Road Parking Lat/Long: 50.7170518, -1.873323
Parking Postcode: BH2 5AA
OS Map grid ref: SZ 090 908

Boscombe Pier Lat/Long: 50.720042, -1.843570
Parking Postcode: BH5 1BN
OS Map grid ref: SZ 111 911

Map: OS Explorer Map OL22 (1:25 000) New Forest

Accessibility

All of the locations are a short easy walk from the car parks. Wheelchair access is possible if you stay on the promenade rather than go down onto the beach. The car parks are pay and display and there is a charge for entering Bournemouth Pier, though the best shots are from the beach rather than the pier itself. There is no admission charge for Boscombe Pier but you will need to check the opening times when planning a visit.

Best Time of Year/Day

Unless you're planning to combine a bit of photography with a family holiday, it's probably best to visit Bournemouth out of season as the beaches can get very crowded. For this reason also sunrise and sunset shoots tend to work best and the sun is in the best position from October to March.

The large sandstone headland of Hengistbury Head and the adjoining Mudeford Spit are located to the east of Bournemouth and form two sides of Christchurch Harbour. Hengistbury Head is an important archaeological site and designated an ancient monument with evidence of human activity dating back 12,500 years.

The area was declared a nature reserve in 1990 and is a Site of Special Scientific Interest for its bird, plant and insect habitats. It was quarried during the Victorian era but the main activity now is tourism, with over a million visitors annually.

Mudeford Spit juts out north of the headland. It is probably best known for its extremely expensive beach huts which change hands for what, in other parts of the country, you might expect to pay for a detached house. From Warren Hill, the elevated part of Hengistbury Head, there are excellent views across to the Isle of Wight, over Mudeford Spit and back along the coast towards Bournemouth.

What To Shoot and Viewpoints

Viewpoint 1 – The Beach

Exit the car park at the south east corner and follow the footpath to the beach. It's a shingle beach which slopes down to the sea. There are many places to stop and shoot along here. You can either use wide angle views and include the waves washing back on forth on the shore for foreground interest, or use the stone groynes. There are good compositions to be had in both directions and evening light enhances the colour of the sandstone headland so that it looks a bit like a less dramatic version of the cliffs at Burton Bradstock (page 192).

Viewpoint 2 – Warren Hill

From the car park follow the footpath to the beach and then the paved track up to Warren Hill. There are excellent views all round from here. Longer focal lengths will enable you to shoot over the beach chalets along Mudeford Spit or back towards Bournemouth. Wide angles will allow use of foreground interest such as the heather in late summer.

Viewpoint 3 – Mudeford Spit

Walk out of the car park at the north east corner and follow the tarmac path to the east. The one mile walk takes you through a wooded area, with occasional views over the reeds towards Christchurch, until you reach the spit. Once here there is a wealth of photographic opportunity – the chalets can be photographed from either side. There are views over Christchurch Harbour or to the Isle of Wight and across the water to Mudeford. It's possible to shoot a variety of compositions with different focal lengths.

Right: Warren Hill from the beach in evening sunlight. Canon 5D, 17-40 at 19mm, ISO 100, 1/5th second at f/16, LEE 0.6 soft grad

How To Get Here

Hengistbury Head is on the coast at the eastern edge of Bournemouth just past Southbourne. From Bournemouth take the A338 Wessex Way heading east. Take the slip road signed to Littledown and the hospital and take the third exit onto Castle Lane East. At the roundabout, go straight ahead into Iford Lane and, at the end, turn left onto Tuckton Lane. At the roundabout take the third exit onto Belle Vue Road. Take the first left onto Broadway and continue on this road until you reach the car park on your right.

Parking Lat/Long: 50.719309, -1.770827
Parking Postcode: BH6 4EN
OS Map grid ref: SZ 164 911

Map: OS Explorer Map OL22 (1:25 000) New Forest

Accessibility

The tarmac path to Mudeford Spit is level and an easy walk. Wheelchair access is possible, though it's about a mile from the car park. During the day there is a land train if you want to take it easy. The walk up to Warren Hill is not arduous and achievable for most people. It's a short, level walk to the beach though once there, wheelchair access is not possible.

Best Time of Year/Day

There are shots to be had at any time of day. Sunsets work well from early September through till late March and good compositions can be found at sunrise throughout the year. Late August/early September is an excellent time to visit as the heather should be flowering then.

Christchurch Harbour from Warren Hill with Mudeford Spit in the distance. Pentax 67II, 45mm f/4, Fuji Velvia 50, LEE 0.9 soft grad

Situated near the boundary between Dorset and Hampshire and with easy access to the New Forest, Christchurch is Dorset's fourth most populated town. Although part of the urban sprawl which extends from Poole into Hampshire, there are some attractive parts of the town with significant historic buildings. The Priory Church is one example; a Grade 1 listed building and the longest parish church in the UK. The castle is also Grade 1 listed, it is a fairly small ruin and is probably of more historic than photographic interest.

The rivers Avon and Stour converge in Christchurch with both the quay and river frontages great places to wander with your camera.

A blue-hour view of Christchurch Priory, from the western side of the churchyard. Canon 1Ds Mk II, 17-40mm f/4L at 22mm, ISO 100, 199 seconds at f/16

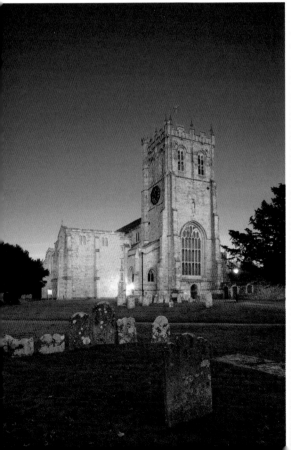

What To Shoot and Viewpoints

Viewpoint 1 – The Priory Church Exterior

The car park in Quay Road is located next to the church. The best angle on the church is probably from the western side of the large churchyard. Headstones can be used for foreground interest, as can the overhanging branches of trees.

Viewpoint 2 – The Priory Church Interior

The building dates from Norman times though has been extensively restored over the years and there is a lot of architectural interest inside. The nave is impressive with heavy, round arches and vaulting.

Viewpoint 3 – The Quay

This is a couple of minutes walk from Quay Road car park. From the Quay there are views along the Avon and the Stour or over towards Christchurch Harbour. It's worth strolling along the riverside but be aware that this is a popular spot with locals and visitors; early morning visits are recommended if you want to avoid getting people in your photos.

How To Get Here

Christchurch is on the coast near the Hampshire-Dorset border about 20 miles south west of Southampton and 5 miles east of Bournemouth. From Bournemouth take the A338 east. Turn off onto the B3073 towards Christchurch. Follow this road to the roundabout which meets the A35 and take the fourth exit onto the High Street. Continue on into Church Street and then turn left onto Quay Road. Follow Quay Road to the car park.

Quay Road Parking Lat/Long: 50.731533, -1.775068
Parking Postcode: BH23 1BY
OS Map grid ref: SZ 159 924

Map: OS Explorer Map OL22 (1:25 000) New Forest

Accessibility

The Priory and the Quay are a very short level walk from the car park and are accessible for wheelchair users. Parking is pay and display and there is a suggested donation for entering the Priory Church. Opening times for the church are 9.30–17.00 Monday to Saturday and 14.15–17.30 on Sundays (subject to services).

Best Time of Year/Day

The Priory photographs well in the evening golden hour and blue hour at any time of year. The Quay is probably best shot at dawn or early morning to avoid the busiest visitor times and the light is best between October and March, when the sun is to the south.

Opposite: The confluence of the rivers Avon and Stour. A dawn shot towards Christchurch Harbour. Pentax 67II, Velvia 50, f/16, LEE 0.9 soft grad

Mudeford was originally a small fishing village at the entrance to Christchurch Harbour but modern development means now it is more or less a suburb of Christchurch. The Quay was constructed in the late 1940s to help combat severe erosion in the area and is now home to a pub, some old fishermen's cottages and a car park. There are ferries to Mudeford Spit (see page 102) and Christchurch (see page 104).

Historically the Haven House Inn and the fisherman's cottages had links with smuggling and in 1784 there was a skirmish between bootleggers and customs officers which became known as the Battle of Mudeford. One customs officer was killed and one of the smugglers later executed for the crime.

These days things are much quieter. There is still a local fishing industry – lobster pots are often piled up on the quay – and it is a base for sailing and windsurfing. Photographically most of the interest is around the quay with the lobster pots and boats in the harbour, and on Avon beach with its wooden groynes and views over to the Isle of Wight and the Needles.

What To Shoot and Viewpoints

Viewpoint 1 – The Quay

It's a very short stroll from the car park to the Quay where there is a lot of interest. You can shoot fishing boats coming and going, use the lobster pots for foreground interest or as subjects in their own right.

Viewpoint 2 – Christchurch Harbour

The section of Christchurch Harbour next to the Quay provides lots of interest. At low tide you can walk out to use the fishing and pleasure boats as foreground in wider views of the harbour and at high tide swans often gather on the water.

Viewpoint 3 – Avon Beach

The beach is at the eastern end of the car park and a promenade takes you past the caravan park. It's possible to walk a long way along the beach to Friar's Cliff. There are wooden groynes for foreground interest and the Isle of Wight beyond makes an excellent backdrop.

Top: Lobster pots on Mudeford Quay, in early morning light. Nikon F90, 24-50mm, Fuji Velvia 50

February sunset at Mudeford Quay on a low tide. Canon 20D, 17-40mm at 17mm, ISO 100, 1/5 second at f/22, LEE 0.9 hard grad

How To Get Here

Mudeford is on the eastern edge of Christchurch, at the entrance to Christchurch Harbour. From Christchurch, take the A35 east towards Lyndhurst. At the roundabout take the third exit onto the B3059 through Purewell. At the next roundabout take the second exit towards Mudeford and drive through the village of Stanpit. Once in Mudeford turn right into Chichester Way and continue to the car park on the Quay.

Parking Lat/Long: 50.724948, -1.741049
Parking Postcode: BH23 4AB
OS Map grid ref: SZ 183 916

Map: OS Explorer Map OL22 (1:25 000) New Forest

Accessibility

All the viewpoints are a short, level walk from the car park and easy for photographers of all levels of fitness. There is good wheelchair access except where you have to get down from the promenade onto Avon Beach.

Best Time of Year/Day

Avon Beach is an excellent sunrise location from September to March. To photograph the sun rising over the Isle of Wight, December, January and early February are the best times. The views over Christchurch Harbour look their best at sunset from mid-October through till mid-February. Shots of the lobster pots and boats in the quay work well at any time.

Top: A fantatsic winter afterglow over Chistchurch harbour at high tide, from Mudeford Quay. Nikon F801s, 24 50mm, Fuji Velvia

A stormy sunset, with swans in Christchurch Harbour, next to the quay.Nikon F4, Fuji Velvia 50, Nikon 24-50mm

Winter sunrise over the Isle of Wight, from Avon Beach. Nikon F801s, Fuji Velvia 50, Nikon 24-50mm, 3-stop grad

Stanpit Village is located on the southern boundary of Mudeford. To its south west is an area of salt marsh that is now the nature reserve of Stanpit Marsh. This marsh has formed from deposits of the Avon and Stour rivers as they meet in Christchurch Harbour. A Site of Special Scientific Interest with both freshwater and saltwater habitats, it is a haven for wildlife.

With over 300 species of bird reported and 14 species of endangered plant, it is an important wetland reserve. Stanpit Marsh is a big draw for bird and nature photographers but there are also landscape opportunities with views over the marshes towards Christchurch Harbour and through the reeds towards Christchurch Priory.

What To Shoot and Viewpoints

Viewpoint 1 – Christchurch Priory

From the car park follow the footpath into the nature reserve. There is a circular walk which takes you across a prototype Bailey bridge over a channel known as Mother Siller's Channel. From here there are shots towards Christchurch and the Priory Church. Reeds growing on the banks of the channel can be used to frame the view or to provide foreground interest.

Viewpoint 2 – Christchurch Harbour

From the southern edge of Stanpit Marsh, there are interesting compositions to be made looking over the reeds and other features towards Christchurch Harbour. The views will vary with the tide but if you can get close to the water's edge on the southeastern tip of Blackberry Point there are good shots of the beach huts on Mudeford Spit.

Viewpoint 3 – Wildlife

There is an abundance of wildlife – especially birds – at Stanpit Marsh including herons, lapwings and greater spotted woodpeckers. There are also numerous species of beetle, many insects and you may be lucky to see and photograph grass snakes.

An early morning view of Christchurch Harbour from Stanpit Marsh. Canon 5D, 17-40mm f/4L at 35mm, ISO 100, 1/13th second at f/16, LEE 0.6 soft grad

Looking towards Hengistbury Head and Mudeford Spit from Blackberry Point. Pentax 67II, 55mm f/4, Fuji Velvia 50

Sunset over Christchurch Priory viewed from Mother Siller's Channel. Pentax 67II, Fuji Velvia 50

How To Get Here

Stanpit Marsh is on the north side of Christchurch Harbour. The car park, next to Stanpit Recreation Ground, is on the right of Stanpit Road as you drive towards Mudeford (p. 106) just past the Ship in Distress pub.

Parking Lat/Long: 50.731534, -1.757421
Parking Postcode: BH23 3ND
OS Map grid ref: SZ 172 924

Map: OS Explorer Map OL22 (1:25 000) New Forest

Accessibility

It is a flat, level walk from the car park along a gravel path which circles around the reserve. This can get wet at high tide and some parts can be rough due to tidal action. Dykes and ditches are often crossed by raised sleeper bridges which can restrict wheelchair access.

Best Time of Year/Day

Good landscapes can be taken all year round as there are compositions in many directions. For sunset shots of Christchurch Priory the summer months are best, and for evening shots over towards Mudeford Spit and the beach huts, October to April can be good. Winter sunrises over Christchurch Harbour also work well. For information about the wildlife on Stanpit Marsh, visit: **www.friendsofstanpitmarsh.org.uk**

Right: A frosty December morning on Stanpit Marsh, looking towards Christchurch Priory. Canon 5D, 24-105mm at 24mm, ISO 100, 0.3 second at f/16, LEE 0.6 hard grad

Poole Harbour at twilight with the town of Poole in the background. A torch was used to paint light onto the boat.

Poole Harbour is famous for being one of the world's largest natural harbours and Sandbanks, on the north entrance of the harbour is infamous for having some of the most expensive real estate in the world.

The harbour was formed at the end of the last ice age and several rivers flow into it, the largest of which is the Frome. It is shallow, with an average depth of 48cm. The entrance – between Sandbanks to the north and Studland to the south – is narrow with a chain ferry running across. Navigation is therefore tricky, especially for the larger boats and ferries that dock at Poole and have to follow a dredged channel through the harbour.

Because of the flat water conditions, water sports such as water skiing, wakeboarding, windsurfing and kitesurfing are popular in Poole Harbour. From the photographer's point of view, participants in the various activities can either be usefully included in the scene to provide some human interest, or make good subjects in their own right.

There are also lots of pleasure and fishing boats in the harbour to provide interest and Sandbanks beach, popular for sunbathing and swimming, is actually quite photogenic.

The best known of the various islands in Poole Harbour is Brownsea Island which is owned by the National Trust and famous as the place where Robert Baden-Powell founded the Scout movement. It is also one of the few places in southern England with a colony of red squirrels. There are trips to the island from Haven Point at Sandbanks.

What To Shoot and Viewpoints

From the car park it's a short stroll across Shore Road to the harbour or in the other direction onto the beach.

Viewpoint 1 – Boats in the Harbour

At low tide, provided you're wearing a good pair of wellies, it's possible to walk quite a long way out into the harbour and get close to the boats. You can fill the frame with them in the foreground or shoot the boats with their reflections in the shallow water.

Viewpoint 2 – Poole Harbour at High Tide

From Shore Road you can shoot across boats on the water towards Poole town or Brownsea Island.

Viewpoint 3 – From Evening Hill

Drive out of the car park and turn right onto Shore Road. Follow it around the shoreline. Where Shore Road becomes Sandbanks Road you start to climb up a gentle slope – Evening Hill. There is roadside parking on the left with views over the harbour towards Brownsea Island. A long, wooden jetty provides interest at the bottom of the frame. This works well with evening side lighting.

Viewpoint 4 – Brownsea Island from Bramble Bush Bay

Cross over to Studland on the ferry and there is a small beach immediately past the toll booth on the right. This is Bramble Bush Bay and is a good spot for shooting sunsets over Brownsea. If you take your car over on the ferry you can park in the National Trust car park on the left, just past the toll booth. If you don't want to get down onto the beach, it is possible to shoot from the roadside near the ferry.

Viewpoint 5 – Sandbanks Beach

Walk onto the beach from the car park. There are lots of possible compositions following the curve of Poole Bay to the east and Bournemouth, or across to Purbeck and Old Harry Rocks. There aren't too many features to include in the foreground, but there are stone groynes to provide some foreground interest.

Opposite top: Sunset over Poole Harbour at high tide. Pentax 67II, 55mm f/4, Fuji Velvia 50, LEE 0.9 soft grad

Opposite middle: Towards Brownsea Island and Purbeck from Evening Hill. Canon 5D Mk II, 24-105mm at 80mm, ISO 100, 10 seconds at f/16, LEE 0.6 hard grad & 1.2 ND, polariser

Opposite bottom: Looking towards Purbeck from Sandbanks beach at sunrise. Pentax 67II, 45mm f/4, Fuji Velvia 50, LEE 0.6 soft grad

Left: Sunset over Brownsea Island from Bramble Bush Bay. Pentax 67II, 45mm f/4, Fuji Velvia 50, LEE 0.9 soft grad

How To Get Here

Sandbanks is on the south eastern corner of the town of Poole. To get to the car park at Shore Road, from Bournemouth head west on the A338 (Wessex Way) towards Poole and take the second exit at the County Gates roundabout onto the Avenue. Follow this road down to Branksome Beach where it turns to the right and up the hill into Canford Cliffs. Turn left at the mini roundabout and follow Haven Road to the end where you will sea Poole Harbour and Brownsea Island in front of you. Turn left and follow Shore Road past the Sandbanks Hotel until you see the car park on the left. To get to the ferry over to Sandbanks and Bramble Bush Bay continue past the car park and go straight across the mini roundabout.

Shore Road Parking Lat/Long: 50.688747, -1.939125
Parking Postcode: BH13 7QD
OS Map grid ref: SZ 043 876

Evening Hill Parking Lat/Long: 50.702291, -1.941568
Parking Postcode: BH14 8LZ
OS Map grid ref: SZ 044 891

Bramble Bush Bay Lat/Long: 50.675605, -1.954233
Parking Postcode: BH19 3BA
OS Map grid ref: SZ 035 863

Map: OS Explorer 118 (1:25 000) Shaftesbury and Cranborne Chase

Accessibility

Each viewpoint is only a short walk from the car – a matter of yards in some cases – and easy for people of all levels of fitness. There are several shooting possibilities from the roadside so good possibilities for wheelchair users.

Best Time of Year/Day

Sandbanks beach looks its best at sunrise and shots are possible all year round though autumn and winter are preferred. You can shoot from Evening Hill at both sunrise and sunset in winter. Late afternoon light suits it most of the year except June and July. You can find suitable compositions for Poole Harbour sunsets at any time of year but summer probably works best. Summer is also the preferred season for shooting sunsets from Bramble Bush Bay, but good shots are certainly possible throughout the year at sunset and in late afternoon/evening light.

Just escaping the clutches of the south coast conurbation, Wimborne Minster is an attractive market town dominated by the twin towers of its Norman Minster church. The town's history dates back to the 8th century and is recorded in the Domesday Book as a small market town. The current population is around fifteen thousand.

The architecture is mainly fifteenth to seventeenth century and thanks to local planning laws is well preserved. The River Stour flows along the outskirts where it meets the River Allen. There are excellent views along the Stour and it is well worth spending some time exploring the walks along its banks.

What To Shoot and Viewpoints

Viewpoint 1 – The Minster

Park in the car park in King Street which is only a short walk from the Minster. There are good compositions possible from both the north and south sides of the church depending on the time of day and year and therefore the direction of light. From the south (King Street) side there is a very effective composition possible, framing one of the towers under the leaves of a tree in the churchyard.

Spring sunrise from the south bank of the Stour by Eyebridge. Pentax 67II, 45mm f/4, Fuji Velvia 50

Viewpoint 2 – The Minster from across the Stour flood plains.

Approaching Wimborne from Dorchester on the A31, instead of turning left at the roundabout onto the B3078 into the town centre, go straight across to stay on the A31 heading east. After a couple of hundred of metres pull into a lay-by on the left. From here there are gaps in the hedges that will allow you a good view across the Stour towards the Minster.

Viewpoint 3 – Eyebridge and The Stour

Eyebridge is a wooden bridge which crosses the Stour. You can shoot symmetrical compositions along the bridge which work especially well at sunrise or along the river from the bridge. The water to the west of the bridge is often very still due to a weir creating perfect reflections in this part of the river. Across the bridge there are some good shots from the banks of the Stour. You can stay on the same side and follow the footpath along the bank in either direction, with plenty of opportunities to stop and take pictures along the way.

Late afternoon in autumn, from the King St. side of the Minster. Canon 1Ds Mk II, 17-40mm at 27mm, ISO 100, 2 secs at f/16

A beautiful spring sunrise reflected in the calm water by the weir next to Eyebridge. Pentax 67II, Fuji Velvia 50, LEE 0.9 soft grad

Eyebridge on a winter morning.
Pentax 67II, 45mm f/4, Fuji Velvia 50, LEE 0.9 soft grad

How To Get Here

Wimborne Minster is 9 miles drive from Bournemouth and 20 miles east of Dorchester. From Bournemouth and Poole head west on the A35 and then take the exit at Upton onto the A350, heading north. At the roundabout, take the third exit onto the A31. Then either:

For **King Street and the Minster**, take the first exit at the next roundabout onto the B3078, go over Julian's Bridge and take the second exit at the mini roundabout into West Street. Follow the one way system and turn left into West Borough (B3078). Turn right into Priors Walk (B3073). Then turn right into East Borough and follow this road as it becomes High Street. At the end of the road turn right into King Street.

For **Eyebridge,** take the first exit at the next roundabout onto the B3078, go over Julian's Bridge and take the first exit at the mini roundabout. Just after the hospital turn left into Cowgrove Road. Go past the turning to Pamphill on the right, and then on the left there is a small, gravelled area where you can park.

King Street Parking Lat/Long: 50.799080, -1.9902420
Parking Postcode: BH21 1EA
OS Map grid ref: SZ 007 999

Stour flood plain Parking Lat/Long: 50.792566, -1.9963521
Parking Postcode: BH21 3DH
OS Map grid ref: SZ 003 992

Eyebridge Lat/Long: 50.800490, -2.007556
Parking Postcode: BH21 4EL
OS Map grid ref: ST 995 000

Map: OS Explorer 118 (1:25 000) Shaftsebury and Cranborne Chase

Accessibility

None of the locations involves much walking and can be easily reached by people of all fitness levels. Getting up onto Eyebridge is not possible for wheelchair users and the footpath to the east of the parking spot at Eyebridge does not have wheelchair access, although heading west the footpath is gravel and is negotiable for wheelchair users.

Best Time of Year/Day

The Minster church can be photographed year round. The north side gets the light in the summer months and the south side during the winter. Viewpoint 2 is best as a sunrise option, especially in the spring and autumn when there may be mist over the flood plains, or in winter when the fields are flooded and colourful skies may be reflected.

Eyebridge and the riverside views nearby – Viewpoint 3 – are probably at their best early in the morning; there are good possibilities year round. As there are more compositional possibilities from the north bank and looking east from the bridge, the best options are probably between October and March, when the sun is rising further south.

Pamphill is a largely unspoilt village with three greens and picturesque seventeenth and eighteenth century cottages. It is part of the Kingston Lacy Estate and has an Arts and Crafts church built in 1907. The Vine Inn is on the Campaign for Real Ale's National Inventory of Historic Pub Interiors.

As well as the buildings there is Abbott Street Copse, a small area of coppiced woodland which is mostly unremarkable apart from its renowned display of bluebells in the spring. Whilst described as 'the best display of bluebells in Dorset,' this is of course highly subjective, Hooke Park in West Dorset (p. 212) may have a better claim to this title.

What To Shoot and Viewpoints

Viewpoint 1 – The Village

From the car park walk along the road towards the village. There is an avenue of oak trees lining the road which is worth a shot in the right light with the village green to either side. The thatched cottages also make good subjects.

Viewpoint 2 – Abbott Street Copse

For most of the year there's probably not much of photographic interest here but it's definitely worth visiting in bluebell season. The bluebell displays are usually very good but can be tricky to photograph as it's not a very 'clean' wood. For the most part it is lacking the rows of straight beech trees which you get in somewhere like Micheldever. If you follow the paths through the copse you will find the odd corner where there is a little more 'structure' and you can always use the paths themselves to add a sense of order.

To get to the copse from the car park walk back along the road and turn left at the T-junction opposite the church. After a couple of hundred metres turn left onto a path (marked as All Fools Lane on the OS map). Two or three hundred metres along here, go through a gap on the right and cross the field to the copse. The route is well marked.

Opposite: One of the pretty, thatched cottages in the village. Pentax 67II, 55mm f/4, Fuji Velvia 50

There are nice displays of bluebells in the copse most years, but the wood is a little untidy and it can be tricky to find a composition with a sense of order. Pentax 67II, 105mm f/4, Fuji Velvia 50

How To Get Here

Pamphill is located about a mile and a half west of Wimborne Minster. From Wimborne leave the town on the B3082 Blandford Road. About half a mile past Queen Elizabeth School, before you reach Kingston Lacy, turn left into Abbott Street. Go past the turning for the farm shop and opposite St Stephen's church, turn left towards Pamphill Village. There is a small car park on the right.

Parking Lat/Long: 50.806284, -2.016296
Parking Postcode: BH21 4EF
OS Map grid ref: ST 984 007

Map: OS Explorer 118 (1:25 000) Shaftesbury and Cranborne Chase

Accessibility

Abbott Street Copse is around half a mile from the car park and the terrain is easy. There are a couple of stiles which mean that wheelchair access is not possible. The walk into the village is not much further but if likely to cause problems, there is another car park further along the road near the school.

Best Time of Year/Day

Abbott Street Copse is best visited in early May for the bluebells, but keep an eye how the flowers are progressing, as this varies slightly from year to year. The cottages look good with spring and summer flowers and the oak avenue is at its most photogenic with fresh green leaves in spring or with autumn colours. These locations can all work at any time of day.

Kingston Lacy is a country house and park near Wimborne, now owned by the National Trust. It was built by the Bankes family who had previously lived at Corfe Castle until its destruction in the Civil War. The house was intended to resemble an Italian Palace.

Kingston Lacy houses important collections of art and antiquities amassed over many years by the Bankes family. As this is National Trust property, you will be bound by the organisation's photography policy (*www.nationaltrustimages. org.uk/photographic-access*) which often does not allow photography inside properties. A tour of the house is well worth the trouble, even if you only take photographs outside.

What To Shoot and Viewpoints

Once outside there is plenty to shoot. Rather than heading for specific viewpoints, spend some time exploring the grounds. As well as shooting the house in the context of the parkland, there are plenty of details to shoot in the 7-acre Japanese gardens, the fernery and the nursery wood, which comes into its own in the summer months with displays of azalea, camellia, rhododendron and flowering cherry trees. In winter, the estate is well-known for its snowdrops.

The whole estate covers 8,500 acres and includes the Iron Age hill fort of Badbury Rings and an extravagant beech tree avenue, originally made up of 731 trees. See next location.

Snowdrops in the garden, with Kingston Lacy House in the background. Pentax 67II, 45mm F/4, Fuji Velvia 50

Opposite: The east elevation of the property. Nikon F4, 24-50mm, Fuji Velvia 50

How To Get Here

Kingston Lacy is about 2 miles west of Wimborne Minster. From Wimborne, take the B3082 Blandford Road. After about 2 miles, turn left into the entrance to Kingston Lacy House and gardens.

Parking Lat/Long: 50.812304, -2.033719
Parking Postcode: BH21 4EA
OS Map grid ref: ST 977 014

Map: OS Explorer 118 (1:25 000) Shaftsebury and Cranborne Chase

Accessibility

There is free parking in the car park but there are entry fees to the house and grounds. The grounds are level, and the terrain is easy; there are signed 1 mile, 2-5 mile walks and 5 mile-plus walks. There are toilets and a restaurant which is open all year. Wheelchair access around the grounds is good though electric wheelchairs and mobility buggies are not allowed inside the house for conservation reasons.

Best Time of Year/Day

The grounds look good in all seasons but are especially popular in summer when the rhododendrons are in flower and in winter when the snowdrops are out. You will need to plan any shoots during visiting hours. For more information, please visit:
www.nationaltrust.org.uk/kingston-lacy

Autumn colours on the beech trees lining the B3082.
Canon 5Ds, 70-300mm f 4-5.6L at 120mm, ISO 100, 0.5 sec at f/16

Badbury Rings is an Iron Age hill fort which now belongs to the National Trust. It is situated about 100 metres above sea level and comprises two main ramparts close together with a third one lower down. It is constructed on an earlier Bronze Age site and was in the territory of a tribe known as the Durotriges, who also built Maiden Castle just outside Dorchester.

There are excellent views all around from Badbury Rings and on a clear day you can see the Isle of Wight. The main photographic interest here is the mile-long avenue of beech trees which flank the B3082 running alongside the ancient monument. The trees were planted in 1835 for Lady Bankes and formed the main driveway to the Bankes's manor house at Kingston Lacy (see page 118). 365 were planted on one side for each day of the year, and 366 on the other, for a leap year.

Unfortunately, many of the trees are dying from old age, disease, climate change and pollution from the heavy traffic and a number have been felled for safety reasons. The National Trust has planted an avenue of Hornbeams to replace the beech avenue which will give the same seasonal colour as the beeches but are more likely to thrive in difficult conditions.

What To Shoot and Viewpoints

Viewpoint 1 – The Hill Fort

From the car park follow the path up to the hill fort. In side lighting there are good shots along the ramparts and closer to the main road. There are trees which photograph well with the fort in the background.

Viewpoint 2 – The Beech Avenue

From the car park walk back to the B3082 and the beech avenue. There are plenty of viewpoints and possible shots in both directions and from either side of the road – just keep walking until you see something. The best compositions are often looking along the road as it goes up over the brow of a hill. Take care when composing to try to achieve separation between the overhanging branches and the road if possible. Also pay attention to the way branches stretch out into the corners of the frame and how trunks help to frame the view beyond. There are a number of road signs and markings which can be distracting; be aware of these and exclude them from the frame if possible.

There are also many possible compositions which don't feature the road; shoot along the canopy of branches on either side of the road, basing your composition around the shapes of branches.

Longer focal lengths (100mm and more on full frame) tend to work best with shots of the beech avenue; the 'compression' effect of telephotos can make it seem almost as if you are looking along a tunnel of trees.

Be aware that the B3082 is a very busy road and cars drive along here very quickly; make sure you are well away from the edge and do resist the temptation to stand in the middle of the road and shoot straight along it. This is not the best composition anyway as it fails to make the most of the undulations in the road.

A tunnel of branches and leaves at the side of the road. Canon 5Ds, 70-300 at 112mm, ISO 100, 1.0 second at f/16

How To Get Here

Badbury Rings is 3.5 miles west of Wimborne Minster. Leave Wimborne, heading west on the B3082 Blandford Road. After about a mile and a half you will see the entrance to Kingston Lacy House on your left and after another mile and a half the turning for Badbury Rings car park is signposted to the right. On the way you will have entered the beech avenue.

Parking Lat/Long: 50.827670, -2.058446
Parking Postcode: DT11 9JL
OS Map grid ref: ST 959 030

Map: OS Explorer 118 (1:25 000) Shaftesbury and Cranborne Chase

Accessibility

You can get good shots of the hill fort and the beech avenue without having to walk far from your car. The grass on the verge can be long and damp, so waterproof boots or wellies are recommended for walking along here.

Best Time of Year/Day

Spring and autumn are favoured seasons for shooting the beech avenue; in spring the fresh, green foliage is impressive and there is often cow parsley growing on the side of the road for additional interest. Autumn colours in the trees can be beautiful and although good shots are possible at any time of day, early morning light streaming through the branches looks especially appealing on a misty morning.

Spetisbury is a 'linear' village with more or less one line of buildings adjacent to the busy A350. Many of these back on to the River Stour which is crossed by the fifteenth century Crawford Bridge. There is a simple iron age fort, Spetisbury Rings, at the south end of the village.

From Spetisbury there is a footpath which runs along the Stour to the village of Shapwick and beyond. There are many photographic opportunities along this walk which are especially suited to winter sunrise photography.

While at first glance Spetisbury might appear to be a rather nondescript ribbon settlement, this area is in fact a very pretty part of the county.

What To Shoot and Viewpoints

Viewpoint 1 – The Village on the Riverbank

From Crawford Bridge shoot north along the river for a view of the houses along the bank; a standard zoom is the best choice of lens for this shot.

Viewpoint 2 – Crawford Bridge

The arched, stone bridge is an excellent subject in its own right. It's possible to get onto the western bank of the river and shoot along the length of the bridge as it stretches across the Stour.

Viewpoint 3 – The Stour

Cross Crawford Bridge to get to the eastern bank of the Stour. After about 25 metres there is a footpath on the right which takes you across fields and along the river bank. There are many places where you can stop and shoot along this footpath.

Opposite: A frosty morning on the banks of the River Stour
Canon 5D Mk III, 16-35 at 25mm, ISO 400,
3.2 secs at f/11, LEE 0.9 hard grad.

How To Get Here

Spetisbury is on the A350 about 3 miles south of Blandford Forum and 6 miles north west of Wimborne Minster. Once in the village turn into the road signposted to 'The Tarrants'; this is on the right if you are approaching from the south and the left if you are coming from the north. Park on this road where it is safe and considerate to do so. If you cross Crawford Bridge there is space for one car on the left about 25 metres past the bridge, opposite the beginning of the footpath described in Viewpoint 3. Take care not to block access to the gate.

Parking Lat/Long: 50.818578, -2.116237
Parking Postcode: DT11 9DP
OS Map grid ref: ST 918 019

Map: OS Explorer 118 (1:25 000) Shaftsebury and Cranborne Chase

Accessibility

Accessibility is excellent for all viewpoints. For Viewpoint 3, the footpath along the Stour, the walk is flat and easy going and you can walk as far as you like. If shooting from Crawford Bridge be aware of traffic; although this is a minor road, it is a popular local cut-through. Wheelchair access to this viewpoint is possible but there is danger from vehicles crossing the bridge. Wheelchair access is not possible to the other viewpoints.

Best Time of Year/Day

Viewpoint 1 is an excellent option for sunrise, especially between April and September. Despite not shooting towards the sun, you should get good light on the houses and it's especially atmospheric with mist on the river. Crawford Bridge works well early morning throughout the year. Views from the banks of the Stour (Viewpoint 3) are best at sunrise and early mornings. Because the river twists and turns, you should be able to find compositions throughout the year, but it works very well in winter with the trees bare and frosty reeds on the river bank.

Medieval Crawford Bridge crosses the Stour at Spetisbury.
Canon 1Ds Mk II, 24-105mm at 24mm, ISO 100,
0.8 sec at f/16, LEE 0.6 soft grad

Horton Tower, near Chalbury Common is a classic example of an eighteenth century folly and was supposedly once the tallest non-religious building in Britain. It was built in 1750 by Humphrey Sturt, Lord of Horton Manor, who was also a Dorset MP between 1745 and 1786.

The tower is a five storey Gothic red brick structure which was probably built as an observatory or as a place where Sturt could observe hunting; from the top there are views for miles around.

It fell into disrepair over the years and all the floors have fallen away and today it is basically a shell. It has recently been given a new lease of life as a place to house mobile phone masts – and some restoration work has been carried out since planning was granted.

What To Shoot and Viewpoints

The tower can be photographed from a distance from the fields just outside the village of Horton or there is a closer view from the top of the hill it stands on. Very close to Horton Tower is All Saints Church at Chalbury which dates from the thirteenth century and is worth making a slight detour for.

Viewpoint 1 – Horton Tower from the Village

As you approach the village from the direction of the Horton Inn (on the B3078), there is turning on the right signposted to Chalbury Common. About 400 yards past this there is a lay-by on the left. Park here and walk further along the road for about 200 yards. Opposite a road on the left there is a gap in the hedge on the right and a stile. Climb over this and follow the marked footpath across the field. You can stop anywhere here for an excellent view of the tower overlooking the surrounding landscape from its commanding position on top of the hill. You will need a long focal length for this – a 70-200mm zoom is ideal.

Viewpoint 2 – The Tower from the Hill

Approaching Horton village from the direction of the Horton Inn (on the B3078), take the right hand turn, signposted towards Chalbury Common. About half a mile up the road on the left is the footpath to Horton Tower. Park safely where you can and follow the footpath for a short distance to the tower – there are possibilities for good compositions on both sides.

Viewpoint 3 – All Saints Church, Chalbury

If you carry on from Viewpoint 2 along the Chalbury Road and fork right just past Tower Close, you will reach the village of Chalbury. The church occupies an elevated position on the left as you drive into the village. It is possible to park on the left just past the church. There are good compositions from the churchyard. The church has medieval windows and a Georgian interior – it's worth taking a look inside.

Opposite: Horton Tower shot from the bottom of the hill in late afternoon sunlight in September (Viewpoint 1). Canon 5D Mk III, 70-200mm f/4L at 140mm, polariser

A lowering sky over All Saints Church, Chalbury (Viewpoint 3). Pentax 67II, 45mm f/4, Fuji Velvia 50, LEE 0.9 soft grad

How To Get Here

Horton is about 5 miles north of Wimborne Minster. From Wimborne head north on the B3078 Cranborne Road. Turn right opposite the Horton Inn and then follow the directions to the individual Viewpoints.

Viewpoint 1 Parking Lat/Long: 50.866669, -1.955140
Parking Postcode: BH21 7JA
OS Map grid ref: SU 032 074

Start of footpath Lat/Long: 50.861647, -1.960896
Parking Postcode: BH21 7EP
OS Map grid ref: SU 028 069

Chalbury Curch Parking Lat/Long: 50.861841, -1.9749507
Parking Postcode: BH21 7EY
OS Map grid ref: SU 018 068

Map: OS Explorer 118 (1:25 000) Shaftsebury and Cranborne Chase

Accessibility

You don't have to walk far from your car to get to any of the viewpoints but the access to Viewpoint 1 involves climbing over a stile and it can be a bit of a scramble if the hedges either side of it are overgrown. Wheelchair access is not possible for Viewpoints 1 and 2. The nearest food and drink is at the Horton Inn on the B3078.

Best Time of Year/Day

As a general rule, buildings in the landscape look their best when side-lit as this helps to reveal their shape and adds depth to the scene. Other lighting can work well, however, for example, strong backlighting can create dramatic silhouettes, especially if there is a colourful sky.

Viewpoint 1 works well late afternoon and in evening light for most of the year. In the winter months the sun sets behind the tower, and in the spring and summer there is sidelighting towards the end of the day. Early morning from this viewpoint provides sidelighting from September to November. In the winter the sun is slightly further round the back of the tower, though still to the side. In summer it is more front-lit from this viewpoint at sunrise.

Viewpoint 2 is a good sunrise and early morning option with sidelighting in the summer and backlighting in autumn and winter. Late afternoon and sunset can work here from October to March.

Viewpoint 3 is best shot from October to March at either end of the day. Interior shots are possible all year round. These work best on overcast days when contrast is less of an issue.

Knowlton is a tiny hamlet north of Wimborne Minster which is home to an extraordinary ruined Norman church situated inside a Neolithic henge monument. The earthworks around the church are obvious but they form only part of a larger complex. Most of the other henges have been ploughed out and are only discernible in aerial photographs. The church was built in the 12th century and was abandoned in the 18th when the roof fell in. The tower is 15th century and made of flint, with bands of stone. It has been suggested that the church at Almer, a few miles away, was built to the same plans and shows what Knowlton church could look like today if it had not fallen into ruin.

The site has a reputation for being haunted and often features in books and newspaper articles about ghosts in Britain. Some visitors claim to be able to feel the sad, macabre atmosphere of the location. For the less sensitive it's enough to experience the peaceful nature of its rural setting.

Haunted or not, it is certainly an intriguing symbol of the transition from pagan to Christian worship and is a location where, in the right conditions, you can take some very atmospheric images.

What To Shoot and Viewpoints

The church generally looks best when given some context and shown within the surrounding henge. It's possible to photograph it from either the western end where the tower is, or from its eastern end. For some reason the western end always seems more balanced. From this end look out for trees and farm buildings poking out from behind the church. Careful positioning and framing is required. Remember that buildings in the landscape appear to have more apparent depth if one side is in shadow.

A dramatic sky is almost crucial to any composition. Contrasty black and white shots can look very effective.

Panoramas work well at Knowlton as you can fully show the earthworks around the church. Canon 5D Mk II, 17-40mm, 1/20 second at f/11, 3-shot horizontal stitch

How To Get Here

Knowlton is about 6 miles north of Wimborne Minster, just off the B3078 Cranborne Road. From Wimborne head north on this road. After about 5 miles you will pass the Horton Inn on your left. The turning for Knowlton church is the next left, about a mile further on. You will see the church on your right, two or three hundred yards along this road and there is a small lay-by with space for three or four cars in front of it.

Parking Lat/Long: 50.891566, -1.968242
Parking Postcode: BH21 5AE
OS Map grid ref: SU 023 102

Map: OS Explorer 118 (1:25 000) Shaftsebury and Cranborne Chase

Accessibility

The church is only a few metres away from the lay-by. The ground is a little uneven in places, but in dry conditions, wheelchair access is possible with assistance. The nearest refreshments are about a mile away at the Horton Inn on the Cranborne Road.

Best Time of Year/Day

Because good compositions are possible from both sides of the church this is a year-round location with possibilities at both ends of the day. Even during the middle of the day dramatic shots are possible. In midsummer the sun rises at a particularly good angle and on winter mornings, frost can add extra atmosphere to the scene.

Evening light at Knowlton; the sidelighting helps to add a 3-D look to the building. Canon 5D Mk II, 17-40 at 22mm, 1/20 sec at f/11

Midsummer sunrise. A small aperture has helped to create a starburst. Canon 5D Mk III, 16-35mm f/2.8L II at 16mm, ISO 100, 0.8 second at f/22, LEE 0.9 soft grad

North Dorset – Introduction

North Dorset has its own distinct character. It is a largely rural area made up of rolling hills and scattered villages including some larger towns such as Blandford Forum and Shaftesbury. The River Stour enters the county in the north and winds its way through the countryside on its way to the sea at Christchurch. Much of North Dorset is in the River Stour Valley, known as the Blackmore Vale.

The chalk plateau of Cranborne Chase extends into Wiltshire and Hampshire. The landscape here is varied with ancient woodland, scarp slopes and hills. There is plenty of archaeological interest with Neolithic and Bronze Age monuments and, on its southern edge, the hill forts of Hambledon Hill and Hod Hill. Cranborne Chase and the West Wiltshire Downs have been designated an Area of Outstanding Natural Beauty.

This part of the county is perhaps less photographed than West Dorset or Purbeck, both of which have more immediately obvious photogenic subjects. But beyond the famous locations of the Hovis Cottages of Gold Hill in Shaftesbury, North Dorset is no less beautiful and well worth exploring with your camera.

Sturminster Newton mill reflected in the River Stour on a summer morning. Canon 5DsR, 24-70mm f/4L at 39mm, ISO 100, 1/25 second at f/11, LEE Landscape Polariser

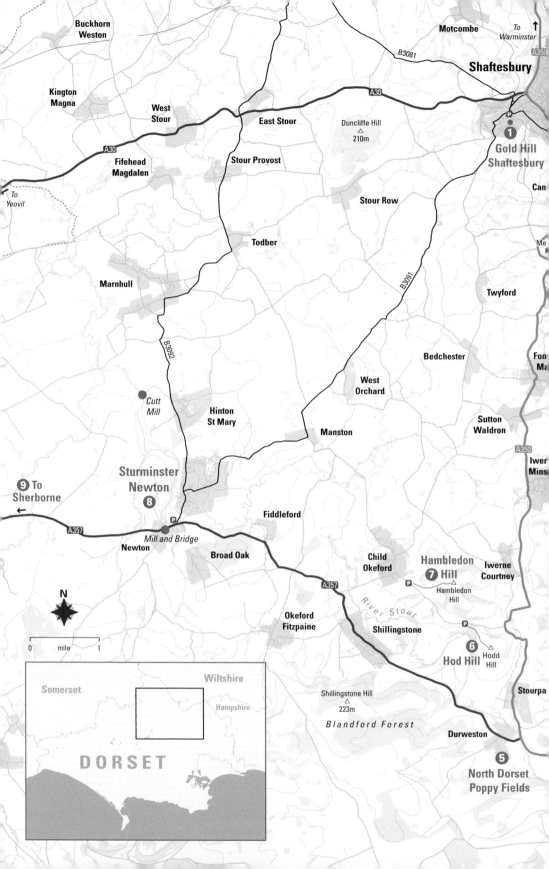

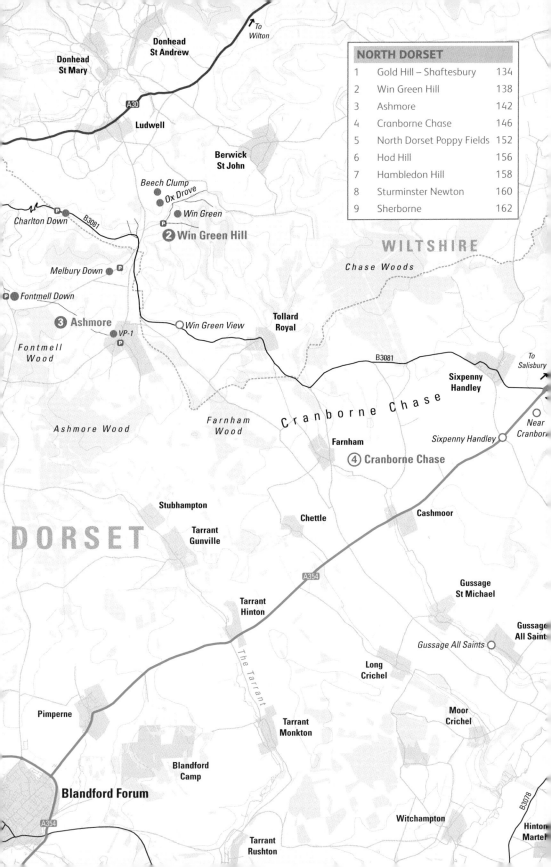

Donhead
St Mary

Donhead
St Andrew

To
Wilton

A30

Ludwell

Berwick
St John

Beech Clump
Ox Drove
Win Green

Charlton Down

B3081

Win Green Hill

Melbury Down

Fontmell Down

Ashmore

VP-1

Fontmell
Wood

Win Green View

Tollard
Royal

WILTSHIRE

Chase Woods

B3081

To
Salisbury

Sixpenny
Handley

Ashmore Wood

Farnham
Wood

Cranborne Chase

Farnham

Cranborne Chase

Sixpenny Handley

Near
Cranbor

DORSET

Stubhampton

Tarrant
Gunville

Chettle

Cashmoor

A354

Gussage
St Michael

Tarrant
Hinton

Gussage All Saints

Gussage
All Saint

The Tarrant

Long
Crichel

Pimperne

Moor
Crichel

Tarrant
Monkton

Blandford
Camp

Blandford Forum

A354

Witchampton

Hinton
Martel

B3078

Tarrant
Rushton

The classic view from the top of Gold Hill, as featured in Ridley Scott's Hovis advert.
Fuji X-Pro2, 18-55mm at 28mm, ISO 200, 1/17 sec at f/8, LEE Landscape Polariser, LEE 0.6 med grad

The hill-top town of Shaftesbury, overlooking the Blackmore Vale, dates back to the 9th century when Shaftesbury Abbey, a Benedictine nunnery was founded here by King Alfred. This became one of the richest religious establishments in the country before being destroyed in the Dissolution, and by the 14th century, Shaftesbury was the most populous town in Dorset. Because the nunnery had the bones of Edward the Martyr it also became a town of pilgrimage.

These days the town is probably best known by tourists and photographers for Gold Hill, a steep cobbled hill descending from the town hall. On one side there are 18th century cottages and on the other, a buttressed stone wall which is part of the remains of the Abbey. The fields of the Blackmore Vale make a wonderful backdrop.

This view was made famous by the 1970s TV advert for Hovis bread by the British director Ridley Scott who went on direct Blade Runner, Alien and more recently The Martian.

What To Shoot and Viewpoints

Viewpoint 1 – Looking down Gold Hill

This is the classic viewpoint and familiar to those who are old enough to have seen the Hovis advertisement. There are not many variations on this composition – you can go slightly wider or slightly less wide, include more of the stone wall on the right or more of the cottages on the

left, but most images will look broadly similar. Your best bet for getting a shot that stands out from the crowd is if your visit coincides with some interesting lighting or weather conditions.

Viewpoint 2 – Looking up Gold Hill

For something different walk down the hill a little way and shoot back up the hill. With the town hall at the top of the hill and the tower of St Peter's Church behind it, this is a very effective shot and it's surprising that it isn't seen more often.

Viewpoint 3 – Park Walk

From the top of Gold Hill walk along Park Lane, which then becomes Park Walk. From here there are fine panoramic views over the parish of St James and the Blackmore Vale.

Looking over the Blackmore Vale from Park Walk. Fuji X-Pro2, 10-24mm at 14mm, ISO 400, 1/45 sec at f/8, LEE Landscape Polariser, LEE 0.6 medium grad

How To Get Here

Shaftesbury is about 20 miles north of Blandford Forum and 18 miles west of Salisbury. From Blandford head north on the A350. As you enter the town take the first exit off the roundabout onto the B3091 (High Street). Stay on this road as it goes through the town. Turn left at the crossroads with Angel Lane and Coppice Street to stay on High Street and follow it round to the right as becomes Bell Street. Bell Street car park (pay and display) is on the left. You may be able to find on street parking in the High Street before you reach it.

From the car park head south along Bell Street and follow it round to the left into the High Street. Here you will see the town hall on the right. Follow the alleyway to the side of the town hall into Gold Hill.

Parking Lat/Long: 51.006704, -2.1941945
Parking Postcode: SP7 8DF
OS Map grid ref: ST 864 230

Map: OS Explorer 118 (1:25 000) Shaftesbury and Cranborne Chase

Accessibility

To get to the top of Gold Hill is a short, easy walk with wheelchair access, but the hill is very steep if you intend to go down (and back up again afterwards!) to photograph it from lower down. There are plenty of places to eat and drink in the town. There are public toilets in the car park.

Best Time of Year/Day

Gold Hill looks best with the light hitting the cottages on the left, which is in the early morning in the winter months and late afternoon / evening in the summer months. The views from Park Walk work well at the beginning and end of the day in the autumn and winter.

Opposite: Looking up Gold Hill. Fuji X-Pro2, 10-24mm f/4 at 17mm, ISO 200, 1/9 second at f/8, LEE Landscape Polariser, LEE 0.6 medium grad

Far-reaching views across the Blackmore Vale from Park Walk. Fuji X-Pro2, 18-55mm at 18mm, ISO 400, 1/40 second at f/8, LEE Landscape Polariser

The classic view from the top of Gold Hill. Fuji X-Pro2, 18-55mm at 28mm, ISO 200, 1/9 second at f/8, LEE Polariser, LEE 0.6 med grad

A winter sunrise, looking north along the Ox Drove.
Canon 1Ds Mk II, 17-40mm at 19mm, ISO 100, 0.3 sec at f/16, LEE 0.9 soft grad

Win Green Hill is in Wiltshire, just over the Dorset border, and is an excellent location worth visiting when you are planning a North Dorset shoot.

Owned by the National Trust and a Site of Special Scientific Interest, Win Hill Green Hill is the highest point on Cranborne Chase giving panoramic views over Wiltshire and Dorset. On top of the hill is a clump of beech trees – typical of the Wiltshire countryside. It's a well-known local landmark and provides an obvious focal point for compositions.

Less well-known is the Ox Drove, an ancient track along which cattle were herded from Devon and Somerset to Hampshire. From the photographer's point of view the track provides a useful way of linking the hills in the rolling countryside of the West Wiltshire Downs.

What To Shoot and Viewpoints

Viewpoint 1 – The Beech Clump

From the car park walk up the gentle slope towards the clump of beech trees. If you need foreground interest, there is a topograph monument and a trig point. Simple compositions with the horizon kept low can be very effective, especially if there is an interesting sky above.

Viewpoint 2 – The Ox Drove

Continue to the top of the hill and walk past the beech clump and you will see the Ox Drove stretching out into the distance along the ridges of the hills. It's not the most distinct of features and benefits from low side lighting to reveal its shape; the added texture of a frosty morning can also help.

Viewpoint 3 – Looking West

Looking to the west, there are views back towards Dorset and the rolling hills of Charlton Down. With longer focal lengths and the right light, it's possible to create bold, layered compositions.

Viewpoint 4 – The Western Slopes

The western slopes of Win Green Hill have some wonderful sharp angles and strong lines, which can be used to create dynamic, geometric compositions. These compositions work especially well in winter, when the bare trees and hedges create a dark outline around the edges of the fields below.

How To Get Here

Win Green Hill is just inside Wiltshire on the border with Dorset, about 4 miles south east of Shaftesbury and 9 miles north of Blandford Forum. From Blandford head north on the A354. After about 5.5 miles, turn left into Millers Lane. Turn left after another half a mile, signposted to Newtown, Ashmore and Shaftesbury. After a mile and a half stay on this road as it bears left and becomes Common Drove. After a further 2.5 miles, turn left at the T-junction onto the B3081. After a mile turn right into Donhead Hollow and then after three or four hundred yards you will see a track on the right, signposted 'By-way to Win Green'. Turn here and follow the track to the car park.

Viewpoint 1 Parking Lat/Long: 50.983398, -2.111876
Parking Postcode: SP7 0EP
OS Map grid ref: ST 923 204

Map: OS Explorer 118 (1:25 000) Shaftsebury and Cranborne Chase

Accessibility

The track to the car park is a bit rough with a number of potholes. Although you don't need a four wheel drive, you do need to take care. From the car park the walk up to the top of Win Green Hill is a short, gentle slope which should pose no problems for photographers of any level of fitness. Wheelchair access is possible.

Best Time of Year/Day

The beech clump photographs well towards the end of the day especially at sunset in the summer months when the direction of the sunlight is to the left and slightly behind it. It's a good sunrise and early morning option all year round with the sun rising more or less behind it in the summer and to the right in winter.

The Ox Drove works well at sunrise throughout the year, though is perhaps best suited to the winter months when low side-lighting helps to pick out the track. For the same reason, shooting it towards the end of the day between April and September is also possible.

Viewpoint 3, looking towards Charlton Down, is best between mid-October and early February when the angle of the sun can help to create a layered look in the hills.

The western slopes of Win Green Hill (Viewpoint 4) are nicely lit at the end of the day throughout the year, but probably look their best on a frosty winter morning.

The beech clump at the top of the hill, with the topograph.
Canon 5D Mk III, 16-35mm at 16mm, ISO 100, 1/30 sec
at f/11, LEE 0.6 hard grad

The western slopes of Win Green Hill on a frosty morning
(Viewpoint 4). Pentax 67II, 55mm f/4, Fuji Velvia 50, 0.9 soft grad

Looking into Wiltshire from Charlton Down on a misty morning.
Canon 1Ds Mk II, 70-200mm f/4L at 109mm, ISO 100, 1.3 seconds at f/16

③ Ashmore

The picture-postcard village of Ashmore, at 700 feet above sea level, is the highest village in Dorset. The village, centred around a pond of possibly Roman origin, is largely unspoilt with 17th, 18th and 19th century houses. There is evidence of a Neolithic settlement here and, being situated on the Roman road from Bath to Badbury Rings, there may have been a Roman military camp and trading post here as well.

In midsummer there is a local folk dance celebration known as Filly Loo whose origins are likely Pagan and celebrate the pond as a source of water. The event was revived in 1956 and takes place on the Friday nearest to midsummer day.

Near Ashmore there are some high viewpoints for shooting the surrounding landscape, including Fontmell Down, Melbury Hill and Charlton Down.

What To Shoot and Viewpoints

Viewpoint 1 – Ashmore Village

You will see the pond in front of you as you drive into the village. You can park on the roadside along the edge of the pond, but be considerate and try to avoid placing your car in a potential composition. There are some beautiful cottages around the pond which on still days are reflected in the ponds.

Viewpoint 2 – Melbury Down

Continue along the road from the airfield and go past the turning to Ashmore. On the left you will see the slopes of Melbury Down. Pull over where it's safe to do so and you will be able to shoot from the roadside.

If you keep going to the end of this road and then do a staggered across into Donhead Hollow, you will get to Win Green Hill.

Viewpoint 3 – Charlton Down

Continue past Viewpoint 2 to the end of the road and then turn left into the B3081. Just over a mile down the road is a lay-by on the left. Park here and from the other side of the road you can shoot across Charlton Down to the West Wiltshire Downs.

Viewpoint 4 – Fontmell Down

Continue along Spread Eagle Hill past the turning for Compton Abbas Airfield and after one or two hundred yards you will see a small car park on the left. From here, there are views over Fontmell Down towards the village of Compton Abbas. There is a footpath across the down into the village.

Cottages reflected in the village pond at Ashmore.
Pentax 67II, Fuji Provia

Winter sunset over Melbury Down.
Pentax 67II, 55mm f/4, Fuji Velvia 50

Above: VP4. Compton Abbas from Fontmell Down.
Canon 1Ds Mk II, 70-200mm f/4L at 200mm, ISO 100, 1/13 second at f/16, LEE 0.6 soft grad

How To Get Here

Ashmore is 7 miles north of Blandford Forum and 4.5 miles south east of Shaftesbury. From Blandford Forum head north on the A350. In the village of Fontmell Magna turn right into Mill Street (signposted to Ashmore). At the end of the road turn left into Spread Eagle Hill and then take the first right, signposted to Ashmore. Drive past Compton Abbas Airfield and turn right again, following the signpost to Ashmore. At the end of the road turn right into North Road and follow this into the village. For the other locations see the directions given in the 'Viewpoint' descriptions.

Ashmore Parking Lat/Long: 50.959498, -2.125201
Parking Postcode: SP5 5AG
OS Map grid ref: ST 912 177

Melbury Down Parking Lat/Long: 50.976024, -2.122733
Parking Postcode: SP5 5AW
OS Map grid ref: ST 914 196

Charlton Down Parking Lat/Long: 50.985758, -2.145838
Parking Postcode: SP7 0DW
OS Map grid ref: ST 898 207

Fontmell Down Parking Lat/Long: 50.967758, -2.163630
Parking Postcode: SP7 0DT
OS Map grid ref: ST 886 187

Map: OS Explorer 118 (1:25 000) Shaftesbury and Cranborne Chase

Accessibility

None of the locations involve walking more than a few metres from your car, so are achievable for photographers of all levels of fitness. Ashmore has good wheelchair access as do the main routes at Fontmell Down. Care should be taken when shooting Melbury Down as you will be parking on the roadside. To shoot from Charlton Down you will need to set up just off the roadside so, again, you will need to be aware of traffic.

Refreshments and toilets are available at the restaurant at Compton Abbas Airfield – a great place for breakfast after a dawn shoot.

Best Time of Year/Day

Ashmore is a great daytime location on still, sunny days as you can get good reflections in the pond. Fontmell Down and Charlton Down are excellent autumn and winter sunrise spots, especially on frosty or misty days. Fontmell Down is also a very good spot for late afternoon and sunset throughout the year. Melbury Down gets side lighting early in the day in the winter months and you can shoot towards the sunset from November to the end of February.

Field of rape seed near Sixpenny Handley. A wide aperture throws the foreground out of focus to create an abstract look.
Canon 5D Mk II, 70-200mm at 200mm, ISO 100, 1/20 sec at f/4, polariser

Cranborne Chase

Cranborne Chase is named after the village of Cranborne with the *Chase* part of the name coming from the hunts which used to take place here. It isn't a single location as such but an area or geographical feature. However, as the landscape has its own distinctive character, it justifies a separate entry.

Cranborne Chase is a chalk plateau of 380 square miles overlapping the borders of Dorset, Wiltshire and Hampshire. It features rolling chalk grassland, ancient woodlands, chalk escarpments, downland hillsides and chalk river valleys. The scenery is at its most dramatic on the Dorset-Wiltshire border with imposing hills and scarp slopes. It is designated an Area of Outstanding Natural Beauty – the sixth largest in the country.

The area is rich in history with many earthworks and archaeology from the Neolithic Age onwards. The Dorset Cursus, a Neolithic monument, runs for about six and a quarter miles through Cranbourne Chase, as does Ackling Dyke, a section of Roman Road.

What To Shoot and Viewpoints

Several locations within Cranbourne Chase, such as Knowlton Church (p. 128) and Win Green Hill (p. 140) are detailed in separate entries, and with such a large area, it is difficult to describe specific viewpoints. However, if you follow the B3081, which runs along the Dorset-Wiltshire border from Shaftesbury to Verwood, there are many places where you can pull over and photograph interesting compositions from the roadside. The area to the east of Win Green Hill and Ashmore (p. 144) has particularly rich photographic potential.

It's also worth driving along the A354 Blandford to Salisbury Road and taking the odd diversion onto the minor roads to villages such as Wimborne St Giles and Gussage All Saints which have attractive churches. Just south of Sixpenny Handley, alongside the A354 is a field with a barn; this is frequently used for growing rape seed and is worth checking out in the spring as the barn makes a great focal point in a sea of yellow rape.

Opposite: On the border of Dorset and Wiltshire on a hazy morning in early spring. Shot from the B3081, east of Win Green Hill. The layers create a sense of depth and the bare tree, silhouetted against the background, makes a strong focal point. Canon 5D Mk II, 70-200mm at 163mm, ISO 100, 1/20th sec at f/16

How To Get Here

A good route to follow is to take the A354 from Blandford Forum heading towards Salisbury. This gives the opportunity to divert off the main road to some of the villages such as Gussage All Saints and Wimborne St Giles, as well as to photograph the rape field near Sixpenny Handley. You will then reach a roundabout where you can turn left onto the B3081 and follow it towards Shaftesbury or turn right and follow the B3081 towards Cranborne.

Win Green Hill view Parking Lat/Long: 50.962257, -2.106972
Parking Postcode: SP5 5QW
OS Map grid ref: ST 925 180

Near Cranborne Parking Lat/Long: 50.932793, -1.958471
Parking Postcode: BH21 5PW
OS Map grid ref: SU 030 148

Sixpenny Handley Parking Lat/Long: 50.938999, -1.999420
Parking Postcode: SP5 5NT
OS Map grid ref: SU 001 155

Gussage All Saints Parking Lat/Long: 50.896575, -2.002887
Parking Postcode: BH21 5ET
OS Map grid ref: ST 998 107

Map: OS Explorer 118 (1:25 000) Shaftsebury and Cranborne Chase

Accessibility

There are many easily accessible viewpoints on Cranborne Chase. Those described are close to the parking spot. Some are close to the roadside so take care when setting up.

Best Time of Year/Day

Good shots are possible on Cranborne Chase at all times of day and year round. The stretch along the Dorset-Wiltshire border is especially suited to dawn and early morning in spring and summer.

Typical rolling chalk downland of Cranborne Chase. Big skies and dappled lighting. Shot just outside Cranborne. Canon 5D Mk II, 24-105mm at 70mm, ISO 100, 1/60 sec at f/11, LEE 0.6 hard grad

Below: The view from the B3081, east of Win Green Hill. The beech clump at the top of Win Green Hill is visible in the distance. Canon 5D Mk II, 70-200 at 104mm, ISO 100, 1/4 second at f/16

The church at Gussage All Saints, one of several pretty villages in Cranborne Chase. Pentax 67II, 45mm f/4, Fuji Velvia 50

Sunset over an opium poppy field near Durweston.
Fuji X-Pro2, 10-24mm f/4 at 10mm, ISO 200, 1/6 second at f/16, LEE 0.9 medium grad

North Dorset Poppy Fields

Summer can be a difficult time for landscape photographers, with early starts, late finishes and harsh light for a large part of the day. In Dorset options are limited further as, for most of the coastal locations, the sun rises and sets over the land. Rather than go into a summer hibernation and wait for the sun to move further south or the leaves to take on autumn hues, there are some fantastic options for summer landscape photography.

Poppy fields are one of them. Poppies are perennial or biennial plants and there are different varieties and different colours. Unfortunately, it is difficult to predict where poppies will grow – unlike bluebells for example, they don't grow in the same place year after year. The seeds can lie dormant for many years and are only triggered into germination when the soil is disturbed and they are exposed to light – when a field is ploughed for example. Poppies usually bloom in June or July but it can be later – some years ago there was a great display of poppies at Fontmell Down in October.

Sunrise over opium poppies near West Morden. Canon 5D Mk III, 24-105mm at 80mm, ISO 100, 1/13 sec at f/16, LEE 0.9 hard grad.

What To Shoot and Viewpoints

You can't predict exactly where poppies will appear but being more rural and agricultural, the north of Dorset is a good bet. You may have to put in a bit of effort and travel a few miles searching for them. In recent years it has become more common for opium poppies to be grown for medical use in this country. Opium poppies have beautiful, pink petals and are grown on the Drax Estate near Wimborne (the fields around East and West Morden are often used) and in the farmland around the village of Durweston. Because of crop rotation however, different fields are used each year.

When you find a poppy field, take great care when photographing it. Do not trample through the middle of the field – stick to the perimeters and defined tracks and do not trespass on private land. Many of the fields have access via public footpaths so check this on an OS map. This is especially true if you find a field of opium poppies. They are a crop and should be treated with the same respect as any other crops.

Getting in close with a wide angle lens and going for extensive depth of field works well, but shooting with a longer focal length and exploiting the 'compression effect' can give the impression of a thick carpet of flowers. Isolating individual flowers with a long focal length and narrow depth of field is also effective.

How To Get Here

Durweston is about 2 miles north west of Blandford Forum. From Blandford head north on the A350 and turn left at the traffic lights, signposted to Durweston. Cross the Stour and take the first left then left again into Church Lane. You can park by the village hall. There are marked footpaths from the village.

Village Parking Lat/Long: 50.874852, -2.201078
Parking Postcode: DT11 0QA
OS Map grid ref: ST 859 083

Map: OS Explorer 118 (1:25 000) Shaftsebury and Cranborne Chase

East and West Morden are about 7 miles south west of Wimborne Minster, just off the B3075 which links the A35 and A31. There are a couple of side roads off the B3075 – follow these and explore the area to see if there are any poppy fields.

Accessibility

Accessibility obviously depends on where you find poppies but there is a good chance you may have to follow footpaths for some distance and the terrain could be uneven.

Best Time of Year/Day

June and July are the best months for finding poppy fields. They can look good at both ends of the day, especially early in the morning with some dew drops on them. Poppy fields can also photograph well in the daytime, especially if there are blue skies and billowing clouds overhead.

Top: Large poppy field above Durweston. Canon 5D Mk II, Zeiss 18mm, ISO 100, 1/20th second at f/6, LEE 0.9 hard grad.

Right: Opium poppies near West Morden. Canon 5D Mk III, Zeiss 21mm f/2.8, ISO 100, 10 seconds at f/22, LEE 0.6 hard grad

⑥ Hod Hill

Managed by the National Trust, Hod Hill is less prominent and less well-known than neighbouring Hambledon Hill but the photographic opportunities it offers are at least as good. It has the largest internal area of any of Dorset's hill forts and, after a steep climb, the views from the top are very rewarding.

It was inhabited by the Durotriges in the Iron Age and then captured in AD 43 by the Romans, who established a camp in the north west corner. Excavations have shown that it was used by around 600 foot-soldiers and a cavalry unit of around 250. It passed out of use around AD 50.

There are double ramparts around the outer edge which are useful for basing compositions around and until around 20 years ago there was a line of silver birches here. These were chopped down by the National Trust in what many photographers probably considered an act of vandalism. The reason was to prevent the roots from destroying the ramparts of this important historical site.

What To Shoot and Viewpoints

Viewpoint 1 – The Ramparts

Once at the top of the hill walk east along the top and you will see fantastic views to the north and east with the double ramparts curving round in front of you. There are many possible compositions, especially shooting towards sunrise when the layering effect of the light can help to increase the perception of depth.

Viewpoint 2 – To the West

From the north west corner of the hill fort there are views west over the Stour towards Shillingstone, which look especially impressive with a low mist in the Stour valley.

Viewpoint 3 – Looking North

The interlocking shapes and folds of the hills looking towards Iwerne Minster make excellent telephoto subjects. Again, early morning mist can create magical effects and enhance the mood.

Summer sunrise over the outer ramparts of the hill fort. Canon 5DsR, 24-70mm f/4L at 35mm, ISO 100 1/10 second at f/11, LEE 0.9 hard grad

An autumn mist in the Stour valley, looking west from Hod Hill. Canon 1Ds Mk II, 70-200mm f/4L at 200mm, ISO 100, 1/8 second at f/11

How To Get Here

Hod Hill is about 3 miles north west of Blandford Forum and 1.5 miles south east of the village of Child Okeford. From Blandford head north on the A350. Go through the village of Stourpaine and after just over a mile turn left, signposted to Child Okeford. A quarter of a mile or so down this road there is a small car park on the left. Park here and then follow the clearly-marked footpath up the hill; you will enter the hill fort at the north west corner.

Parking Lat/Long: 50.900233, -2.210072
Parking Postcode: DT11 8PS
OS Map grid ref: ST 853 112

Map: OS Explorer 118 (1:25 000) Shaftsebury and Cranborne Chase

Accessibility

It's a short, but very steep climb to the top of the hill, which requires a moderate level of fitness. Wheelchair access is not possible. Refreshments are available from pubs in nearby Child Okeford or Stourpaine.

Best Time of Year/Day

Hod Hill looks best with low side-lighting revealing its shape and form. This is best achieved early or late in the day between April and October. In spring and early autumn there is a good chance of mist here in the Stour valley.

The hills to the north of Hod Hill on a misty morning.
Canon 1Ds Mk II, 70-200mm f/4L at 82mm, ISO 100, 2.5 seconds at f/16, LEE 0.6 soft grad

More prominent than its close neighbour Hod Hill (previous pages), Hambeldon Hill has been described as the most impressive Iron Age hill fort in Dorset. It was acquired by the National Trust in 2014 and has multiple ramparts and wonderful views over the Blackmore Vale and into Wiltshire and Somerset. It is one of the best preserved hill forts in Britain as well as being a Site of Special Scientific Interest and a National Nature Reserve. There are many rare species of plant and animal to be found here, including 28 species of butterfly.

There is some historical interest from the Civil War; the Clubmen made their last stand on Hambledon. They were a group of country folk who resented the looting carried out by both sides in the war. They banded together armed only with clubs and carried banners proclaiming: 'if you offer to plunder or take our cattle, be assured we will bid you battle.' Between two and four thousand of them fought against Cromwell at Hambledon in August 1645. They were routed and most fled.

There are lots of curves in the ramparts to help create dynamic compositions. Canon 5Ds, 16-35mm f/4L at 25mm, ISO 100, 1/15 second at f/11, LEE 0.6 medium grad

What To Shoot and Viewpoints

Impressive as it is to the naked eye, Hambledon Hill can be a difficult place to photograph and definitely benefits from being shot in the right conditions – low side lighting really helps to reveal the form and lines of the ramparts, giving more depth and coherence to compositions.

There are no specific viewpoints to aim for as such. Once at the top of the hill, walk along the ramparts and look for interesting compositions. Some will be more obvious such as wide angle shots with the ramparts sweeping through the shot – it's possible to find some nice curves and 'S' shapes to lead through the frame. There are lots of other possibilities – use longer focal lengths to pick out geometric patterns formed by the interaction of the lines of distant ramparts or zoom in on the trees in the fields below the hill. These fields have good potential on misty mornings, with the tops of the trees poking out above a low-lying mist. Although it's not easy carrying everything up the hill, you will appreciate having a full range of focal lengths with you.

The western side of the hill is probably the more photogenic with its clearly-defined ramparts, but this is not to say the other side should be ignored – it's certainly a good option on a misty morning.

Opposite bottom: There is plenty of opportunity to pick out lines and angles with longer lenses. Canon 5Ds, 70-300mm f/4-5.6 at 79mm, ISO 100, 0.3 second at f/13

A late summer's evening, looking south along the ramparts on the west of Hambledon Hill. Nikon F4, Fuji Velvia 50

How To Get Here

Hambledon Hill is about 4 miles north west of Blandford Forum, overlooking the village of Child Okeford. Follow the directions to Hod Hill (page 156) and continue past the car park in the direction of Child Okeford. About a mile further on, just past the sign welcoming you to the village, there is a lay-by on the right with space for about four cars. Park here, and then walk a few yards along the road towards the village. Just past a small terrace of houses there is a gravelled track, which is a bridleway. Follow this track – be careful not to follow the marked footpath next to it, which will take you into the village.

After about 100 metres you will enter some woodland. Where the path bends to the right there is a gate into a field with a National Trust sign and a rather worrying notice warning of a bull in the field. Go through this gate and walk up to the top of the hill.

Parking Lat/Long: 50.908441, -2.230286
Parking Postcode: DT11 8ET
OS Map grid ref: ST 839 121

Map: OS Explorer 118 (1:25 000) Shaftsebury and Cranborne Chase

Accessibility

It's a steep climb to the top of the hill which requires at least a moderate level of fitness. Wheelchair access is not possible. There is a pub in Child Okeford.

Best Time of Year/Day

It's possible to shoot at Hambledon Hill year round. With the western slope of the hill being the most photogenic, afternoon and evenings suit this location best, especially towards the end of the day with the sun low in the sky picking out the details of the ramparts. The views from the eastern side can be good early in the day, especially on misty mornings.

Sturminster Newton – the 'capital of the Blackmore Vale' – is a sleepy town which holds a market on Mondays. This used to have one of the largest cattle markets in England but it closed in 1998. The larger part of the town, Sturminster, lies to the north of the River Stour with Newton, the smaller part, to the south.

The main photographic interest is the mill, one of several flour mills built on the River Stour. It is an L-shaped building, partly 17th-century stone and partly 18th-century brick. It lies about 300 metres upstream of an impressive six-arch medieval bridge. By following the footpath upstream from the mill it will take you to Riverside Villas where the Dorset novelist Thomas Hardy lived when he wrote *The Return of the Native*.

What To Shoot and Viewpoints

Viewpoint 1 – Sturminster Newton Bridge

From the car park walk towards the bridge. There are some good angles to shoot it from the side of the river.

Viewpoint 2 – Sturminster Newton Mill

From the car park walk along the main road towards the bridge. Cross the bridge and then immediately on your left is a footpath which takes you along the river to the mill. There is a weir which means that the water in front of the

mill is usually still, with good reflections. There are plenty of reeds for foreground interest. For a different composition, try taking a low viewpoint and framing the mill with reeds.

Viewpoint 3 – Cutt Mill

A mile and a half north of Sturminster Newton is the village of Hinton St Mary. Beautifully situated on the banks of the Stour is Cutt Mill. Its origins are unclear but the present stone dates from the 18th, 19th and 20th centuries. Unfortunately, the building is in a sad state of repair following a fire in 2003. Nevertheless, it makes a nice focal point for a photograph looking up the river from the bridge.

Top left: Sturminster Newton mill, reflected in the River Stour on a summer morning. Canon 5DsR, 24-70mm f/4L at 39mm, ISO 100, 1/25 second at f/11, LEE Landscape Polariser

Top right: Because of the angle of sunrise, the mill is usually regarded as a summer location. Even though the sun is not at the ideal angle in winter – there is no direct light falling on the building – in the right conditions, excellent shots are possible. Canon 1Ds Mk II, 17-40mm f/4L at 20mm, 0.8 second at f/22, LEE 0.9 soft grad

Bottom left: Sturminster Newton Bridge on a frosty morning. Canon 1Ds Mk II, 70-200mm f/4L at 200mm, ISO 100, 1/15 second at f/11

Bottom right: The last light of the day hitting Cutt Mill in December. Canon 1Ds Mk II, 17-40mm f/4L at 22mm, ISO 100, 2 seconds at f/16, polariser

How To Get Here

Sturminster Newton is 9 miles north west of Blandford Forum and 9 miles south west of Shaftesbury. From Blandford head north on the A350 towards Shaftesbury. At the traffic lights turn left onto the A357. Go through Durweston and Shillingstone and after 5 miles you will be approaching Sturminster Newton Bridge. On the right, opposite Common Lane and The Bull Tavern is a small car park.

For Cutt Mill cross over Sturminster Newton Bridge and continue through the town on the B3092 until you reach Hinton St Mary. Turn left into Marriage Lane which bears sharp left and becomes Cutt Mill Lane. At the end of the lane is the mill, with parking for around six cars. The last section of the lane is steep and if it is icy, park further up and walk down to the mill.

Sturminster Newton Parking Lat/Long: 50.921298, -2.306581
Parking Postcode: DT10 2BS
OS Map grid ref: ST 785 135

Cutt Mill Lat/Long: 50.948070, -2.319414
Parking Postcode: DT10 1NG
OS Map grid ref: ST 776 165

Map: OS Explorer 129 (1:25 000) Yeovil and Sherborne

Accessibility

It's a short, level walk from the car park to the viewpoints which should present no problems for any fitness level. There is no disabled access to the banks of the river to photograph the mill.

Best Time of Year/Day

Most shots of Sturminster Newton mill are taken early in the day in summer when the sun falls nicely onto the building. However, it does also shoot well in winter, especially on frosty mornings when you can make the most of the reeds in the foreground. The bridge is a good early morning subject year round.

Cutt Mill is a good late afternoon and sunset location year round, though especially around midsummer when you can shoot directly towards the setting sun. From midsummer through until early autumn, the early morning light can also be quite flattering.

⑨ Sherborne

Sherborne has been described as the most attractive town in Dorset. Some of the buildings date back to the 15th century and it has retained its historical charm, free from ugly modern development. The beautiful abbey church, referred to as Sherborne Abbey, with its vaulted ceiling is very photogenic. Many of the buildings, including the Abbey, are constructed of hamstone an ochre-coloured stone from Somerset.

There are two castles in Sherborne. The old castle was built between 1107 and 1135 and was bought by Sir Walter Raleigh in the 16th century. He attempted to convert it into a house but gave up in the 1590s and built the new castle. The old castle was ruined by the Parliamentarians at the end of the Civil War. Raleigh was sent to the Tower and executed by James I. The new castle was then bought by the Digby family, who still own it. The 30 acres of gardens were landscaped by Capability Brown. There are excellent views of the castle both from the gardens and across the lake.

What To Shoot and Viewpoints

Viewpoint 1 – The Abbey

The nearest car park to the Abbey is Culverhayes in Ludbourne Road. Exit the car park onto Ludbourne Road and turn right at the end and then left into Half Moon Street. You will see the Abbey on the right with the green in front of it. A good angle to shoot the abbey is from the western side of the green towards Abbey Close. There are often cars parked to the left of it which can make clean compositions difficult, as do the many passers-by. It's best to visit early morning or evening.

Stormy light inside the old castle.
Canon 1Ds Mk II, 17-40mm f/4L at 19mm,
ISO 100, 1/20 second at f/16

The abbey church in the blue hour.
Canon 5DsR, 17mm TSE, ISO 100, 20 seconds at f/8

Viewpoint 2 – The Almshouse

St John's Almshouse is located on the south west corner of the green. This is a beautiful building with an oriel window and a cloister, and can be photographed from the street.

Viewpoint 3 – Sherborne New Castle

Approaching Sherborne from the south via the A352, turn right into the B3145, New Road. As the road bends round to the left you will see the entrance to the castle on the right. There is a lot to see in and around the grounds of the castle so it's good for exploring. Photography is not permitted inside the castle.

Viewpoint 4 – Sherborne Old Castle

Carry on along New Road past the new castle and turn right at the end, then immediately right into Castleton Road. The old castle is at the end of the road and parking is available for visitors. There are some good compositions of the crumbling castle with a backdrop of mature trees.

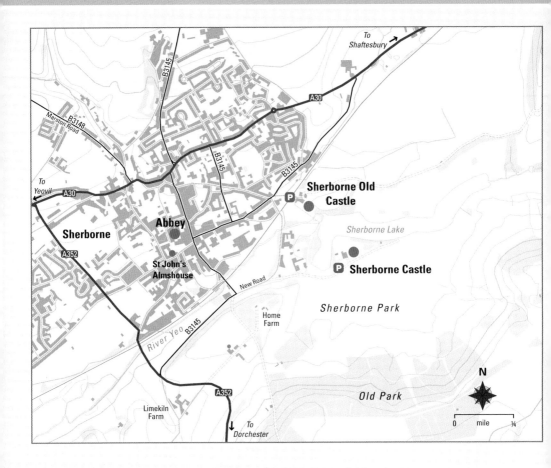

How To Get Here

Sherborne is about 16.5 miles north of Dorchester and 5 miles east of Yeovil. From Dorchester take the A37 towards Yeovil and then turn right onto the A352. You reach Sherborne in about 15 miles. The best route into the town is probably to turn off into the B3145 and then follow the signs into the town centre. This route will take you past the turning for Sherborne Castle and is also convenient for getting to the Old Castle (see above).

Culverhayes Car Park Lat/Long: 50.946646, -2.512173
Parking Postcode: DT9 3ED
Parking OS Map grid ref: ST 641 164

Sherborne Castle Lat/Long: 50.946038, -2.500656
Sherborne Castle Postcode: DT9 5NR
Parking OS Map grid ref: ST 649 164

Sherborne Old Castle Lat/Long: 50.948826, -2.503665
Sherborne Old Castle Postcode: DT9 3SA
Sherborne Old Castle OS Map grid ref: ST 647 167

Map: OS Explorer 129 (1:25 000) Yeovil and Sherborne

Accessibility

None of the viewpoints are physically demanding and wheelchair access is good.

Best Time of Year/Day

Both the Old Castle and New Castle are closed in the winter. See their respective websites for details of entry times:

www.sherbornecastle.com

www.english-heritage.org.uk/visit/places/sherborne-old-castle

A visit as late as possible in the year will increase your chances of some atmospheric lighting and fewer visitors.

Sherborne Abbey is best visited between November and February when there will be early and late sun to warm the stonework. Dawn may be better than sunset as there will be fewer people around. The abbey is floodlit in the evenings, so good for blue hour shots.

Opposite: St John's Almshouse, showing the cloister.
Fuji X-Pro2, 10-24mm f/4 at 10mm, ISO 400, 1/250 second at f/8

West Dorset – Introduction

West Dorset is classic Thomas Hardy country with rolling hills and dramatic sea cliffs. These include the golden cliffs at West Bay and Burton Bradstock, made famous in the TV series Broadchurch. This region officially has its eastern boundary at Dorchester, where the council is based, and continues to Lyme Regis in the west, and the border of Devon.

West Dorset is an area of contrasts. Parts of it feel very remote and isolated, for example Eggardon Hill has an atmosphere of wilderness, totally removed from the modern world yet is only minutes off the A35, the main road through the county. On the other hand there are pretty, thatched villages, the regency resort of Lyme Regis and the town of Bridport, nicknamed 'Notting-Hill-on-Sea' because of the trendy Londonites who have moved to the area.

This part of Dorset has lots of history. Lyme Regis and Charmouth are important sites for fossils and some of the most important finds in the UK have been along this stretch of coast. A near-complete ichthyosaurus found here is now on display in the Natural History Museum. There are also Iron Age Hillforts such as Pilsdon Pen, which at 910 feet, is the second highest hill in Dorset. More recently, Tolpuddle is famous as the birthplace of the Trade Union movement.

The West Dorset coastline has its own distinctive character. It is home to Golden Cap, the highest sea cliff on the south coast, and also the unique Chesil Bank, a 17-mile stretch of pebbles connecting the Isle of Portland to the mainland. The shingle beach runs from Portland to West Bay and forms a spit from Abbotsbury to Portland, behind which lies The Fleet, the largest inland lagoon in Britain.

Evening light on St Catherine's Chapel with the Fleet and Chesil Bank behind.Canon 1Ds Mk II, 70-200mm f/4L at 109mm, ISO 100, 1/5 second at f/11, polariser

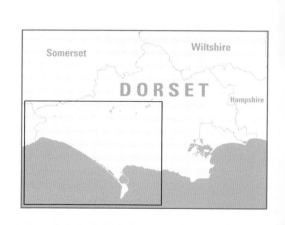

① River Frome

The river Frome is a true Dorset chalkstream, rising at Evershot in the Dorset Downs and 30 miles later running into the English Channel at Poole Harbour. On its journey it passes through some classic Dorset countryside and the towns of Maiden Newton, West Stafford, Dorchester, and Wareham. East of Dorchester it runs over sand, clay and gravel, resulting in the flood plains near Wareham.

There are several places along the route of the Frome where it's worth stopping to take shots including Wareham Quay (see page 40), Stinsford (where Thomas Hardy's heart is buried in the churchyard), Tincleton and Lower Bockhampton.

What To Shoot and Viewpoints

Viewpoint 1 – Tincleton

The village of Tincleton is little more than a collection of cottages with a reasonably attractive church but, just around the corner, there is a lovely spot to photograph the Frome. Approaching from the east, drive through the village and turn left into Watery Lane. After about half a mile there is a bridge over the Frome with a lay-by on the right just before it. The view upriver is lovely, especially in spring with cow parsley on the banks. Standard zooms are ideal for this view.

Viewpoint 2 – Lower Bockhampton

Continue west of Tincleton on Islington Road for about 3 miles and then turn left into Bockhampton Road. After less than half a mile you will reach the village of Lower Bockhampton. It's a little tight, but some on-street parking is possible in places. Continue through the village and you reach an attractive brick bridge. There is a path alongside the river and, from here, there are shots of the bridge looking towards the village and along the river. Again, a standard zoom is probably the best option for shots at this viewpoint.

Viewpoint 3 – Lewell Mill Farm, West Stafford

Park considerately near West Stafford village hall and continue on foot.The road bends to the right in front of the village hall and then left. After about 350 yards turn left into the drive of the Dairy House (marked as 'The Manor House' on the OS map) and immediately right through a metal gate onto the marked footpath. Follow this footpath across fields to Lewell Mill Farm where you turn left and cross a bridge. There are views upriver which although not dramatic, are certainly pretty – classic 'Hardy Country'.

A swan on the Frome near Lewell Mill Farm (VP 3).
Canon 5D, 24-105mm f/4L at 55mm, ISO 100,
1/4 second at f/16, LEE 0.6 soft grad

How To Get Here

Tincleton is 5 miles east of Dorchester and about 15 miles west of Poole. From Poole take the A35 heading west towards Bere Regis. Just as you reach the village of Bere Regis take the first exit at the roundabout, then turn left onto Southbrook which then becomes Rye Hill. After 2.5 miles turn right and then after another 2.5–3 miles go straight across the crossroads and carry on to Tincleton. Follow the directions in Viewpoint 1 to get to the viewpoint.

Tincleton Lat/Long: 50.717982, -2.3279884
Parking Postcode: DT2 8AU
Parking OS Map grid ref: SY 769 909

Lower Bockhampton is 3 miles west of Tincleton.

Lower Bockhampton Lat/Long: 50.715425, -2.396984
Parking Postcode: DT2 8PZ
Parking OS Map grid ref: SY 720 907

West Stafford is 2.5 miles east of Dorchester. Heading west on the A35, past the roundabout where you turn off for Stinsford and Kingston Maurward, turn left onto the Alington Avenue, the B3144. Take the second exit at the roundabout onto the A352. Take the first exit at the next roundabout then the first turning on the left and follow this road into West Stafford. On-street parking is possible near the Village Hall if you park considerately.

West Stafford Lat/Long: 50.705342, -2.387936
Parking Postcode: DT2 8AG
Parking OS Map grid ref: SY 727 895

Map: OS Explorer Map OL15 (1:25 000) Purbeck and South Dorset

Accessibility

Viewpoint 1 is just a few yards from the parking spot. Disabled access is possible but full access may be tricky because of fences and gates.

Viewpoint 2 is also easily accessed, though how far you have to walk depends on where you are able to park your car. There is easy access onto the path but width may restrict wheelchair access.

Viewpoint 3 is a level walk from the village and should present no problems for anyone with a moderate level of fitness but there is no disabled access.

Best Time of Year/Day

These views look their best in spring when there are fresh, green leaves on the trees and cow parsley on the banks of the river. Viewpoint 1 works well early on in the day, especially if there is some mist rising from the river Viewpoints 2 and 3 work well in the late afternoon and early evening when there is light on the bridge at Viewpoint 2 and the river banks at Viewpoint 3.

Top: VP1. A light mist rises from the Frome on a spring morning near Tincleton. Pentax 67II, 55mm f/4, Fuji Velvia 50, f/16, LEE 0.6 soft grad.

Bottom: VP2. Across the bridge at Lower Bockhampton. Pentax 67II, 55mm, Fuji Velvia 50, f/16, polariser & LEE 0.9 soft grad.

Osmington Mills is a coastal hamlet 5 miles north east of Weymouth. Its rocky beach and bay are very beautiful and provided inspiration for the landscape painter John Constable who honeymooned in the area in 1816.

The village itself is very pretty and the local pub the Smugglers Inn, which dates back to the 13th Century, was the home of Emmanuel Charles, the leader of the most notorious gang of smugglers in the area during the early 19th century. This traditional pub is a great place to stop for a pint and a bite to eat after a hard afternoon's photography, and if you spend the same or more as your parking ticket the landlord will reimburse you.

What To Shoot and Viewpoints

Viewpoint 1 – The Eastern Bay

From the car park follow the footpath around the back of the pub and then down onto the beach. There are lots of large, round pebbles on the beach to provide foreground interest for compositions, both towards Weymouth and Portland and east towards Ringstead Bay. East-facing compositions can work well at sunset as well as sunrise as the stones and cliffs can take on a golden hue in the evening light.

Viewpoint 2 – The Western Bay and Waterfall

It's possible to walk from the car park down to the shore but, due to coastal erosion this is no longer an official route. Instead follow the footpath around the back of the pub as above, and then walk along the shore to the waterfall that tumbles over the small cliff. If you get in close with a wide angle you can make it look more dramatic than it is to the naked eye. This works especially well if you photograph it towards the rising sun in the winter months.

Opposite top: Golden light on a spring evening, looking east on the western half of Osmington Mills Bay. Canon 20D, 17-40mm f/4L at 17mm, ISO 100, 0.3 second at f/22, polariser, LEE 0.6 soft grad

Opposite bottom: The Waterfall on the beach at Osmington Mills. Nikon D300, 10-20mm at 16mm, ISO 200, 1.6 seconds at f/29, polariser. © Ross Hoddinot

The Smugglers Inn at Osmington Mills. Fuji X-Pro2, 10-24mm at 18mm, ISO 400, 1/400 second at f/11

How To Get Here

Osmington Mills is a 7 mile drive from Weymouth and is 6 miles south east of Dorchester. From Weymouth take the B3155 east out of town and then at the roundabout take the second exit onto the A353. Continue through Preston and after about two miles turn right onto Mills Road. Follow the road for about a quarter of a mile to the car park opposite the Smugglers Inn.

From Dorchester take the B3144 south out of town and then take the A352 south towards Broadmayne and Warmwell. After about 9 miles take the third exit on the roundabout at Warmwell onto the A353. After 2.5 miles turn left onto Mills Road and follow this to the car park.

Smugglers Inn Car Park: When you pay for parking they reimburse your ticket if you spend the same amount or more in-house. Parking is £5 for 3 hours.

Parking Lat/Long: 50.634896, -2.376171
Parking Postcode: DT3 6HF
Parking OS Map grid ref: SY 734 817

Map: OS Explorer Map OL15 (1:25 000) Purbeck and South Dorset

Accessibility

It's an easy walk down to both sides of the bay, though there is no disabled access. Because of the rocky shore, wearing walking boots with good ankle support is recommended.

Best Time of Year/Day

It's possible to shoot at Osmington Mills throughout the day but the most atmospheric shots will be in the early morning and evening, from mid-October through till mid-February.

Early morning sun lights up Weymouth Harbour in August.
Canon 5DsR, 16-35mm at 19mm, ISO 100, 1/15 sec at f/11, polariser

Situated at the mid-point along the Jurassic Coast, Weymouth is Dorset's third largest town and was one of the first modern resorts. It was popularised by King George III who spent his summers there between 1789 and 1805. Apart from the royal connection, the town's biggest claim to fame is probably that it appears to be where the Black Death reached England in 1348. More recently, Weymouth – along with Portland – played host to the sailing events of the 2012 Olympic Games.

Despite a general atmosphere of faded grandeur, the Georgian seafront is attractive, curving around the sheltered bay. The inner harbour, near the town bridge, is also appealing with charming early 19th century houses, fishing boats and pleasure craft. The adjacent marina is usually full of expensive-looking boats.

It might seem odd to find a nature reserve almost in the heart of the town, but to the north is the RSPB reserve of Radipole Lake – an oasis of calm where it is possible to forget that you are so close to a bustling resort. Among the reeds here are waders, warblers and wildfowl, as well as dragonflies, butterflies and the occasional otter.

What To Shoot and Viewpoints

Viewpoint 1 – The Seafront and Beach

From the car park by the Pavillion walk along the esplanade for a few hundred metres. In the stretch before the pier bandstand you can photograph from the beach, the terraces of houses and hotels to the left towards Bowleaze Cove and the coast stretching around to Osmington Mills.

Viewpoint 2 – The Harbour

From the same car park by the Pavillion, walk away from the seafront to Custom House Quay. From here you can photograph the pretty cottages on the south side of the harbour. Across the town bridge you can shoot Custom House Quay, or find compositions on both sides of the harbour from the bridge itself.

Viewpoint 3 – Radipole Lake

Radipole Lake is next to the Swannery car park near the station in town. From the seafront turn into King Street, the B3155, and turn right into Radipole Park Drive. A footpath wanders amongst the reeds and lagoons leading to a viewing shelter and a hide, all within easy walking distance of the visitor centre.

Morning sun lights up Weymouth Harbour. August. Canon 5DsR, 16-35mm at 22mm, ISO 100, 1/15 second at f/11, polariser

How To Get Here

Weymouth is about 7 miles south of Dorchester and 25 miles west of Bournemouth. From Dorchester head south on the A354 and from Bournemouth or Poole head towards Dorchester on the A35. Take the first exit onto the A354 at the roundabout by Tesco. Follow the A354 into Weymouth and then take the second exit at the roundabout, staying on the A354. Take the second exit again at the next roundabout, staying on the A354. Then at the next roundabout, take the first exit onto Dorchester Road, the B3159. At the end turn right onto the Esplanade, B3155, and continue along to the car park at the Pavillion. You may see some parking on the seafront on your way past – take note of any parking restrictions: usually for permit holders only.

For directions to Radipole Lake, see Viewpoint 3.

Pavillion Parking Lat/Long: 50.609611, -2.447307
Parking Postcode: DT4 8EA
Pavillion Parking OS Map grid ref: SY 684 789

Map: OS Explorer Map OL15 (1:25 000) Purbeck and South Dorset

Accessibility

All of the locations are a short, easy walk from the car. There is wheelchair access for all the viewpoints though it may not be possible to get down onto the beach. Shots are however possible from the esplanade.

Best Time of Year/Day

The bay is east-facing so shots of the beach and seafront work well early morning all year round. Shots of the south side of the harbour are best at dawn or early morning from April to September. For Custom House Quay the light will suit it best at the end of the day from early October to early February. Blue hour shots of the harbour will work well at any time of year and sunrise shots from the town bridge are possible from late February to late March.

Winter sunrise on Weymouth Beach, looking towards the Pier Bandstand. Canon 1Ds Mk II, 17-40mm at 17mm, ISO 100, 0.3 second at f/16, LEE 0.9 soft grad.

Weymouth Harbour, morning in August. Canon 5DsR, 24-70mm f/4L at 59mm, ISO 100, 1/15 second at f/11, polariser

Winter sunrise, with the lighthouse viewed from the west.
Canon 5D Mk III, 16-35mm f/2.8L at 20mm, ISO 100, 13 seconds at f/11, LEE 0.6 hard grad & LEE 1.2 ND

④ Portland

The tied island of Portland – connected to the mainland only by the shingle spit of Chesil Bank – lies just south of Weymouth. It is best known for Portland stone which has been used in many famous buildings including St Paul's Cathedral and the UN headquarters in New York, and quarrying remains an important industry today.

Portland Harbour is one of the largest man-made harbours in the world and was built between 1848 and 1905. Originally a naval base which played an important role during the First and Second World Wars, it is now a civilian port and is a popular area for water sports, hosting the sailing events for the 2012 London Olympic Games.

The island is famous for its classic red and white striped lighthouse at Portland Bill – an important landmark for ships passing the headland and its notorious tidal race.

From Portland Heights you get a wonderful view along Chesil Bank whilst north of Portland Bill is Church Ope Cove – a beach littered with quarry debris, now worn into beautifully rounded pebbles.

What To Shoot and Viewpoints

From the car park at Portland Bill, the lighthouse is obvious towering above it. There are viewpoints to the east and west.

Viewpoint 1 – From the East

From the car park walk east past the Lobster Pot café. There are several points where you can stop and shoot back towards the lighthouse but the best view is probably from the rocky outcrop which has a winch for lowering the fishing boats onto the water. From here you can shoot over the rocky ledges towards the lighthouse. A variety of compositions are possible: portrait and landscape orientations or including and excluding the edge of the ledge in the foreground. There are also good viewpoints from the ledges between here and the lighthouse and, at low tide, down on the shoreline.

Viewpoint 2 – From the West, by Pulpit Rock

Walk to the right of the lighthouse from the car park and turn to the west towards Pulpit Rock. As you get near Pulpit Rock you will see two or three spots where there is a gentle slope down to the rocky ledge below. Take care walking down to it as there are loose rocks and it is easy to slip. You can set up right next to Pulpit Rock and shoot towards the lighthouse, over the waves breaking on the rocks below. Again, a variety of compositions is possible, even without having to move your tripod. Both long and short exposures look good – short exposures can be impressive with big waves crashing on the rocks, or longer shutter speeds can lead to an ethereal look.

Viewpoint 3 – Pulpit Rock

Pulpit Rock is a rock stack which is the remains of a natural arch that was cut away by quarrymen in the 1870s. The ledge which it is best shot from is to the west

Winter sunrise, viewed from the east. Canon 5D Mk II, 24-105 at 24mm, 25 secs at f/11, polariser, LEE 0.6 hard grad

The view over Chesil Bank from Portland Heights at dusk.
Nikon Df, 24-120mm at 82mm, ISO 200, 2.5 seconds at f/11

of the car park and involves a bit of scrambling over rocks, but no serious climbing. It is possible to walk onto the ledge from Pulpit Rock itself but the path is very narrow, with a sheer drop to the – often rough – sea below. It's not for the faint-hearted or vertigo sufferer. There are many compositional possibilities, mostly involving using the natural lines of rock ledges to lead the eye to the stack.

Sea spray can be a real problem from this viewpoint so make sure you have a lens cloth and some cleaning fluid to keep your lens and filters clean, and keep a constant eye on them to ensure they are clean.

Viewpoint 4 – Church Ope Cove

North east of Portland Bill, near the Portland Museum, is Church Ope Cove. On the way to Portland Bill, you will go through Pennsylvania Road. Park at the (free) Church Ope Cove car park on this road then walk left out of the car park. After 50 metres cross the road into Church Ope Road, next to the Portland Museum. Walk to the end of the road and follow the path and steps down to the cove. Once on the shore, the round pebbles make excellent foreground interest for general views of the bay.

Viewpoint 5 – Portland Heights

On the way to Portland Bill turn left at the roundabout by the Portland Heights Hotel and park in the free car park. From here it is a walk of a couple of minutes to the viewpoint with Chesil Bank stretching out below.

Pulpit Rock at sunset. Fuji X-E1, 10-24mm at 10mm, ISO 200, 7.5 seconds at /16, LEE 0.6 hard grad and LEE 1.2 ND

By the end of August, the sun is rising round the headland at Church Ope Cove.
Canon 5DsR, 16-35mm f/4L at 16mm, ISO 100, 4 seconds at f/11, LEE 0.9 medium grad & 3-stop ND

How To Get Here

Portland Bill is 7 miles south of Weymouth. From Weymouth take the A354 through Wyke Regis and across to the Isle of Portland, through Fortuneswell and Easton and along to Portland Bill.

Portland Bill Parking Lat/Long: 50.515427, -2.456609
Parking Postcode: DT5 2JT
Portland Bill Parking OS Map grid ref: SY 677 684

Church Ope Cove Parking Lat/Long: 550.53983, -2.431551
Parking Postcode: DT5 1HT
Pavillion Parking OS Map grid ref: SY 695 712

Portland Heights Parking Lat/Long: 50.557010, -2.437533
Parking Postcode: DT5 1LF
Pavillion Parking OS Map grid ref: SY 687 729

Map: OS Explorer Map OL15 (1:25 000) Purbeck and South Dorset

On the beach. Chesil Beach detail. Canon 5DsR, 17-40mm f/4L
at 25mm, ISO 100, 1/40th second at f/11, polariser

Accessibility

The view of the lighthouse from the east involves an easy, level walk of just a couple of minutes from the car park but it's not really wheelchair friendly. To get to the viewpoint from the west and for Pulpit Rock it is no further, but requires some scrambling over loose rocks and is not recommended for those with limited mobility. There is no wheelchair access.

The walk down to Church Ope Cove is an easy 400 metres or so and there are steps down to the shore and again, no wheelchair access.

The viewpoint at Portland Heights is very close to the car park and is accessible for wheelchair users.

The Lobster Pot café by the lighthouse is open year round and serves very good food.

Best Time of Year/Day

Good shots can be had at Portland Bill all year round and throughout the day. It is an especially good bad weather location or 'grey day' option if you enjoy long exposure photography. The western viewpoint for the lighthouse works well as a winter sunrise and Pulpit Rock is a good sunset spot from mid August through till late March. Excellent blue hour and night shots of the lighthouse are also possible. Being east facing, Church Ope Cove is especially well suited to sunrises.

Anglers silhouetted against the sunset on Chesil Beach at West Bexington.
Canon 1Ds Mk II, 24-105mm at 105mm, ISO 100, 1/4 sec at f/16, LEE 0.6 soft grad

Chesil Beach, also known as Chesil Bank, stretches for **17 miles** from Portland to West Bay. The beach is a shingle ridge which connects the Isle of Portland to the mainland. The stones are naturally graded, getting smaller in size the further west you head. It is said that locals can tell their location by the size of the stones. The brackish lagoon behind Chesil Beach between Portland and Abbotsbury is known as the Fleet. Bird life along the beach is plentiful with herons, little egrets and warblers. You get great views of Chesil Beach and the Fleet from both Portland Heights (see page 180) and Abbotsbury Hill (see page 188).

There are several spots along Chesil Beach where it's worth stopping to take photos including Chiswell on Portland, at the very start of the Beach and West Bexington, just west of Abbotsbury.

What To Shoot and Viewpoints

Viewpoint 1 – Chiswell / Chesil Cove

From the car park just off the roundabout where Portland Beach Road meets Victory Road, you will see the shingle ridge of Chesil Cove right in front of you. Climb up the ridge and to your left you will see the cliffs of West Weare and to your right, Chesil Beach stretches out into the distance. There are often boats here at Chesil Cove which make good foreground interest for shots in either direction along the beach, or you can go for a more minimalist approach; this location is excellent for layered compositions comprising simple bands of shingle, sea and sky.

Viewpoint 2 – West Bexington

The car park is right on the beach at West Bexington, making this one of the least taxing locations in the book. There are views west towards the cliffs at Burton Bradstock, making this a great option for sunset. It is popular with anglers and the shingle shelves steeply down to the sea here. One possible composition is to shoot from the bottom of the slope and silhouette fishermen standing on the ridge at sunset.

How To Get Here

Chiswell / Chesil Cove is on the northern end of Portland, just where Chesil Beach joins onto the island. From Weymouth take the A354 to Portland. On Portland Beach Road, at the third roundabout, instead of taking the first exit onto Victory Road and up through Fortuneswell to Portland Heights, turn right into the entrance to the pay and display car park.

Parking Lat/Long: 50.563496, -2.450785
Parking Postcode: DT5 1AL
Parking OS Map grid ref: SY 681 738

West Bexington beach is halfway between Abbotsbury and Burton Bradstock, about 5 miles from each village. From Weymouth take the B157 coast road for 22 miles and turn left into Beach Road. Continue along Beach Road for about 4 miles until you reach the car park. From Dorchester, follow the A35 west towards Bridport. Turn left into the B3159, going down the hill just before the road bends right into Winterbourne Abbas (signposted towards Winterbourne Steepleton). Turn right to stay on the B3159 and then left onto Coombe Road. Go through Portesham and turn right onto Goose Hill, the B3157. Stay on the B3157, through Abbotsbury. About 4 miles past Abbotsbury, turn left into Beach Road and down to the car park at West Bexington Beach.

Parking Lat/Long: 50.676008, -2.665040
Parking Postcode: DT2 9DG
Parking OS Map grid ref: SY 530 864

Map: OS Explorer Map OL15 (1:25 000) Purbeck and South Dorset

Accessibility

Chiswell/Chesil Cove: It is a steepish but short walk from the car park up over the ridge onto the beach at Chesil Cove. Walking any distance on the shingle can be tiring. Wheelchair access is not possible up the shingle slope.

West Bexington: Step off the car park onto the beach. Access is possible for all levels of fitness, though again, walking on the shingle can be heavy going and wheelchair access across the stony beach is not really possible. Some shots are possible from the car park itself.

Best Time of Year/Day

Chiswell/Chesil Cove: Shooting long exposures and minimalist black and white works well at any time of day or year in the right conditions, i.e. overcast with textured skies. For colour images, sunset shots are possible from mid-October to mid-February, but best from November to the end of January.

West Bexington: The sun never quite rises or sets completely over the sea here, but good sunsets are possible from early October to late Feburary. From mid-November to mid-January there are also opportunities for sunrise shots.

*Chesil Cove will appeal to fans of long-exposure minimalist
Canon 5D Mk II, 17-40mm F4L at 40mm, ISO 10
180 seconds at f/22, B+W 10 stop N*

The picture-postcard village of Abbotsbury is the kind of place people conjure up in their minds when they first think of Dorset, with thatched cottages and stone houses, many of which date back to the 16th century. The village is about a mile from the coast on a stretch of Chesil Bank including the western end of the Fleet Lagoon.

A popular location with tourists, it is best known for its swannery and sub-tropical gardens. The abbey was destroyed in the Dissolution, though some buildings remain, notably the barn and the 14-century St Catherine's Chapel. The latter probably survived because it was useful as a beacon for sailors.

What To Shoot and Viewpoints

Viewpoint 1 – St Catherine's Chapel from Abbotsbury Hill

Drive west out of the village up Abbotsbury Hill, the B3157. Pull into the second lay-by on the left and cross the road to take the footpath up the hill. From here there are various places where you can set up and shoot the chapel with the Fleet and Chesil Bank behind it.

Viewpoint 2 – The Fleet Lagoon

Drive through the village and take the left turn into Cleverlawns, signposted towards Abbotsbury Sub Tropical Gardens. Follow the road to the end where there is a car park. From the car park there is a boardwalk up onto Chesil Beach. Head east and you will see the western end of the Fleet. There are views along the lagoon or across the lagoon towards the chapel.

Viewpoint 3 – Chesil Bank

There are excellent views along Chesil Bank itself, either to the west or the east, or if you enjoy minimalism, a simple three-layer shot of shingle beach, sea and sky.

How To Get Here

Abbotsbury is about 9.5 miles south west of Dorchester, about a mile inland from the coastline of Chesil Bank. From Dorchester take the A35 west towards Bridport. Just before Winterbourne Abbas, turn left into Coombe Road, the B3159. Keep straight on towards Portesham, down Portesham Hill and turn right into Goose Hill, the B3157. Follow this road into Abbotsbury. From here you can drive through the village and up Abbotsbury Hill, or turn left towards Chesil Bank.

Lay-by on Abbotsbury Hill Lat/Long: 50.672522, -2.623529
Lay-by on Abbotsbury Hill Postcode: DT3 4LA
Parking OS Map grid ref: SY 560 860

The Fleet Parking Lat/Long: 50.659573, -2.623510
Parking Postcode: DT3 4LA
Parking OS Map grid ref: SY 560 846

Map: OS Explorer Map OL15 (1:25 000) Purbeck and South Dorset

Accessibility

The footpath to Viewpoint 1 is gentle and does not require a high level of fitness but is not suitable for wheelchair users. The walk from the car park to Chesil Bank is short and easy along the boardwalk, but walking on shingle can be heavy going and tiring, especially for anyone with mobility issues. There is no wheelchair access.

Best Time of Year/Day

The view of St Catherine's Chapel from Abbotsbury Hill works particularly well as a winter sunset with side lighting giving depth to the scene and revealing the shape of the building. This shot is viable from late September through till mid-March. In late spring and summer the rising sun does a similar job, lighting the front of the chapel but leaving the side in shadow, creating depth. This is possible from April until mid-August. Afternoon and sunset shots of the Fleet and Chesil Bank work well in winter from November to mid-February, and in mid-winter, sunrise shots along Chesil Bank can also be effective.

View west along Chesil Bank at sunset. Canon 1Ds Mk II, 17-40mm at 21mm, ISO 100, 3.2 seconds at f/22, LEE 0.6 hard grad

VP1. Evening light on St Catherine's Chapel, with the Fleet and Chesil Bank behind. Crop from Canon 1Ds Mk II, 70-200mm f/4L at 109mm, ISO 100, 1/5 second at f/11, polariser

Looking across the Fleet towards St Catherine's Chapel. Canon 1Ds Mk II, 24-105mm f/4L at 58mm, ISO 100, 1.3 seconds at f/6, polariser

Quiet is the word that springs to mind when visiting Littlebredy (a.k.a. Little Bredy). This small village sits at the head of the Bride Valley surrounded by the Dorset Downs. The village itself is quaint and old-fashioned with thatched cottages. The River Bride begins at Bridehead House where a lake has been formed by damming the springs which are the source of the river. The river then tumbles over a small waterfall from the edge of the lake.

As you travel along the Bride Valley beauty abounds with rolling hills topped by clumps of trees. To the south of the parish is the Valley of Stones National Nature Reserve, a site of early human occupation in Dorset. The reason for its name comes from the large stones scattered on the slopes of the downs. Legend has it that these were left there by two giants playing stone-throwing games. The geological explanation is a little more mundane: they are the result of thawing at the end of the last ice age which caused sandstone on surrounding hilltops to break up and slump downhill.

What To Shoot and Viewpoints

Viewpoint 1 – The Waterfall and Lake

From the parking spot by the decorative bus shelter walk downhill along the private road into the village. Turn left at the village hall onto a path and walk alongside the church and into the grounds of Bridehead House – a sign welcomes visitors, although public access is not possible to the entire grounds. You will see the waterfall and artifical lake in front of you.

Once at the waterfall, choosing the right viewpoint with a wide lens can make it look a little more impressive than it is in reality. At the right time of year you can use the colourful, fallen leaves for foreground interest.

If you follow the river away from the waterfall you will find another part of the village tucked away, with some pretty, thatched cottages, which are worth a discreet shot or two. You can then turn right and walk up the hill back to your car.

Viewpoint 2 – The Bride Valley

Continue west on Longland's Lane, turn left at the end into Abbotsbury Lane and then right into Cox's Lane and continue along the Bride Valley. There are several places where you can stop and follow footpaths into the hills or even get good shots from the side of the road – there are some excellent spots along this first section of the drive, before you reach Abbotsbury Lane. If there is broken cloud above, then dappled lighting can help to add depth to the hilly landscape, and clumps of trees make strong background focal points.

Viewpoint 3 – The Valley of Stones

Walk from the parking spot back the way you came into the village, but fork right rather than left up the hill, back towards the A35. You will walk along a lane which twists and turns and takes you past the entrance to Bridehead House. About half a mile along this lane, where it bends round to the left, there is a clearly-marked footpath on the right which takes you through the valley. This is classic rolling Dorset countryside with plenty of opportunities to stop and take pictures.

How To Get Here

Little Bredy is about 6.5 miles west of Dorchester. From Dorchester head west on the A35 and after about 5 miles turn left into Longland's Lane. Follow this to Littlebredy. Just past the private road which leads to the river and the main collection of cottages, there is an ornamental bus shelter. It is possible to pull over and park safely just past this.

Parking Lat/Long: 50.700069, -2.585722
Parking Postcode: DT2 9HH
Parking OS Map grid ref: SY 587 891

Map: OS Explorer Map OL15 (1:25 000) Purbeck and South Dorset

Accessibility

It's a short stroll from the parking spot to the waterfall and artificial lake, achievable for all levels of fitness, but is not really possible for wheelchair users because of the narrow path alongside the church. Depending on how far you walk along the footpath through the Valley of the Stones, a reasonable degree of fitness is required.

Best Time of Year/Day

The waterfall looks its best in the autumn, with some colour on the trees surrounding it and photographs well towards the end of the day so that you're not shooting into the sun. The Bride Valley and Valley of Stones also suit an autumn afternoon, with low sun raking across the landscape.

Above: One of the pretty riverside cottages at the bottom of the village. Fuji X-Pro2, 18-55mm f/2.8, ISO 400, 1/640 second at f/8.0

Top: Dappled sunlight on the hills flanking the Bride Valley, near Long Bredy. Canon 1Ds Mk II, 24-105mm f/4L at 28mm, ISO 100, 1/10 second at f/16, LEE 0.6 hard grad

Left: The waterfall at Bridehead. It's not a big waterfall, but a low viewpoint and wide angle composition can make it look more imposing. Canon 1Ds Mk II, 17-40mm f/4L at 17mm, ISO 100, 0.6 second at f/22, polariser

The beach at Burton Bradstock is another of West Dorset's classic locations. This marks the start of Chesil Beach, which is attached to the land here and is near where the River Bride flows into the sea. The sandstone cliffs have been eroded as at nearby West Bay with the same 'honeycomb' appearance. Like the neighbouring cliffs they also glow golden in low sun. There is a bed of ammonites in a layer of rock at the top of the cliffs and, following rockfalls, these can often be found on the beach.

This section of the coastline is prone to landslips and you should stay well away from the cliffs. Tragically, there was a fatality here in 2012 when a young woman was buried under falling rock while walking along the beach. There have been several sizeable landslips since the incident, so this is not a warning to be taken lightly.

What To Shoot and Viewpoints

There are fabulous views along the cliffs in both directions – the trick is to be here at the right time.

Viewpoint 1 – Ledges by Freshwater Beach

From the National Trust car park at Hive Beach, walk west towards Freshwater Beach by the mouth of the

Burton Cliff near Freshwater Beach. Canon 5D, 17-20 at 21mm, ISO 100, 2 secs at f/16, LEE 0.6 soft grad

River Bride and the large holiday park. At low tide there are some rocky ledges visible, although this does depend on recent weather and how much shingle has been washed up over them. When they are visible, they make excellent foreground interest with the cliffs reflected in the rockpools. Take a low viewpoint to make the most of them and maximise depth of field by setting the hyperfocal distance. From here you can also shoot with longer lenses towards the cliffs at West Bay.

Viewpoint 2 – Looking along Chesil Beach

From closer to the Hive Beach car park you can shoot along the shingle beach in either direction. Fallen rocks can make good foreground interest but also serve as a reminder of how unstable the cliffs can be.

Viewpoint 3 – Minimalist Compositions

Burton Bradstock is another location where simple pictures work well. In the right conditions, you can simply shoot straight out to sea with no focal point, manufacturing some foreground interest by photographing the backwash of waves.

How To Get Here

Burton Bradstock is on the coast, 13 miles west of Weymouth and 9 miles east of Lyme Regis. Head out of Weymouth on the A354 and turn left at the roundabout onto the B3157. Stay on the B3157 all the way to the outskirts of the village and then turn left into Beach Road. Follow this road down to the beach and there is a National Trust car park (pay and display, free for members) on the left.

Parking Lat/Long: 50.696766, -2.721631
Parking Postcode: DT6 4RF
Parking OS Map grid ref: SY 491 888

Map: OS Explorer Map OL15 (1:25 000) Purbeck and South Dorset

Accessibility

It's a very short stroll to the beach from the car park but walking along to the ledges near Freshwater Bay is heavy going. Fortunately good shots are available from Hive Beach if you don't fancy trudging across the pebbles. Wheelchair access is not possible onto the beach. The Hive Beach Café opposite the car park is a very good for refreshment.

Best Time of Year/Day

Sunset shots are possible from mid-October to mid-February and the ideal time is midwinter when the sun is setting over the sea. It's not really a sunrise location but this can be done in mid-winter, with the sun rising over Portland in the distance. It is definitely a low-tide location: not only is it at its most photogenic with the tide out, but much safer. With a high tide you'll find yourself walking close to the base of the cliff. It is essential to check the tide times and heights when planning a shoot here and make sure that you leave the beach before the tide starts coming back in.

Burton cliffs glowing gold in evening sun. Canon 5D Mk II, Zeiss 21mm f/2.8, ISO 100, 15 seconds at f/22, polariser & LEE 1.2 ND

The cliffs at West Bay from Freshwater Beach. Canon 5D Mk II, 24-105 at 80mm, ISO 100, 13 secs at f/16, LEE 0.6 soft grad, 1.2 ND

Crepuscular rays over the sea at Burton Bradstock. Canon 5D Mk II, Zeiss 21mm f/2.8, ISO 100, 3.2 seconds at f/22, LEE 0.6 hard grad & 1.2 ND

The setting sun casts its golden glow on East Cliff, from the harbour wall.
Canon 5D Mk II, 24-105mm f/4L at 28mm, ISO 100, 30 seconds at f/16, Polariser, LEE 1.2 ND

West Bay was originally known as Bridport Harbour and was established to export that town's principal products of rope and nets. When the railway arrived in 1884 it was renamed West Bay and attempts were made to turn it into a resort, but it remains small – a village-sized resort, whose other main activity is fishing.

West Bay is best known for the dramatic East Cliff, a vertical honeycomb-textured sandstone cliff which is constantly being eroded. From early autumn through till early spring, the setting sun lights the cliff, giving it a golden glow. The view along the shore to Burton Bradstock is one of the best on the Dorset coast.

The BBC series *Harbour Lights*, filmed in the late 1990s and early 2000s, was in a fictionalised version of the town. More recently, the ITV series *Broadchurch* was filmed here. The latter was a big hit and has had a significant effect on visitor numbers to the area.

What To Shoot and Viewpoints

Viewpoint 1 – East Cliff from the Harbour Wall

From the car park walk past the Bridport Arms on your left and onto the eastern wall of the harbour. From here there are excellent views across to East Cliff.

Depending on where you position yourself you can use the waves washing on the shore as foreground interest or the rocks below the harbour wall. Moderate wide angles of around 28–35mm are recommended for this composition. Alternatively, a short telephoto focal length can be used for a closer view of the cliffs.

Viewpoint 2 – The Western Harbour Wall

For long exposure fans, the western wall of the harbour makes an excellent subject. If you prefer really minimalist compositions, the marker for the eastern side of the harbour can be shot with a lot of space around it.

Viewpoint 3 – East Cliff from the Beach

From the car park walk directly south, past the Bridport Arms on your right, onto the shingle beach. Walk along the beach for a closer view of the cliffs. Foreground interest can be provided by the waves crashing onto the shore or by rocks on the beach.

Viewpoint 4 – The Harbour

Cross the road from the car park and you will find yourself on the harbour's edge. This is a proper harbour, with fishing boats bobbing around. These can make great subjects on a sunny afternoon while you're waiting for the golden light of evening to hit East Cliff.

Fishing boats in the harbour on a sunny afternoon. Canon 5D Mk II, 24-105mm f/4L at 29mm, polariser

A ghostly fisherman stood still for around half of this exposure on the western harbour wall at dusk. Canon 5D Mk II, 24-105mm at 58mm, ISO 200, 93 secs at f/11, LEE 0.6 hard grad & Big Stopper

A closer view of the cliffs from the beach. Canon 1Ds Mk II, 17-40 at 20mm, ISO 100, 0.8 second at f/16, polariser

How To Get Here

West Bay is 1.5 miles south of Bridport and 14 miles west of Dorchester. From Dorchester take the A35 west towards Bridport. After 12 miles you enter the outskirts of Bridport. Take the first exit at the roundabout continuing on the A35. After half a mile take the second exit at the next roundabout onto West Bay Road. Go straight over the mini-roundabout and continue on West Bay Road, following it as it bends round to the right past Station Road. Turn left into the pay and display car park in front of the Bridport Arms.

Parking Lat/Long: 50.710656, -2.761671
Parking Postcode: DT6 4EN
Parking OS Map grid ref: SY 462 904

Map: OS Explorer 116 (1:25 000) Lyme Regis and Bridport

Accessibility

The harbour and the beach are a very short, level walk from the car park. The harbour and harbour walls can be accessed by wheelchair users. The beach is more problematic for wheelchair users; it is shingle, which can also be hard work if you are walking any distance. Behind the beach the cliffs are very unstable and there have been several large landslides here and at Burton Bradstock in recent years – do not stand or sit at the base of the cliff. There are several pubs and cafés in the town for refreshments.

Best Time of Year/Day

This is very much an afternoon and evening location. Sunny afternoons really suit shots of the harbour and as the sun gets lower in the sky, golden light on the sandstone cliffs can be magical. Shots of the cliffs at sunset are possible from early September to early April, but the best shots are in late autumn and winter when the sun sets at right angles to East Cliff. High tides work best.

The shingle beach at Eype Mouth is located by a natural break in the Jurassic Coast cliffs where the River Eype reaches the sea. Eype is old English for 'a steep place' and the approach to the beach is indeed along a narrow, steep lane. There are sandstone cliffs both to the east and west but the best views are probably to the west, with Thorncombe Beacon towering above its surroundings. Interesting rocks on the shore can add immediate interest to your shots.

What To Shoot and Viewpoints

The beach is accessed from near the car park entrance.

Viewpoint 1 – To the West

From various points along the beach there are good compositions looking west. Have a walk along the beach looking for suitable foreground interest; there is plenty, from where the Eype drains into the sea, all the way to the cliffs at the far end, where there are some interesting rocks on the foreshore. Get in close to foreground interest with wide angle lenses to exaggerate linear perspective, or use the natural curves of the beach to lead the eye through the shot. This viewpoint is one which will look best towards the end of the day.

Viewpoint 2 – To the East

At the start of the day, especially in winter, when the sun rises over the sea there are lots of possibilities shooting in the other direction, along the cliffs to the east. Again, seek out some suitable foreground interest and get in close with wide angle lenses.

Viewpoint 3 – Minimalism

This is a great location for playing with minimalism. You can shoot the waves washing around the rocks dotted along the shoreline, or keep things even simpler, with a view out to sea across the shingle.

Viewpoint 4 – Clifftop Views

From the car park there is a footpath heading west along the cliffs. There are excellent views from along this path looking up Thorncombe Beacon or back inland towards the villages of Lower and Higher Eype.

How To Get Here

Eype Mouth is about 16 miles west of Weymouth, a couple of miles south west of Bridport and nearly 7 miles east of Lyme Regis. From Bridport take the A35 west. After about a mile, turn left into New Street Lane, signposted towards Eype. As the road bends around to the right turn right into Mount Lane, signposted toward Lower Eype and the beach. Follow Mount Lane to the bottom of the hill and you will find the car park on the right. The car park is privately owned and there is an honestly box when nobody is there to collect fees.

Parking Lat/Long: 50.716469, -2.783924
Parking Postcode: DT6 6AL
Parking OS Map grid ref: SY 447 910

Map: OS Explorer 116 (1:25 000) Lyme Regis and Bridport

Accessibility

Getting down onto the beach is easy and requires no great level of fitness but there is no disabled access. Walking along the shingle can be tiring, but you don't need to go far. The walk up to Thorncombe Beacon is a steep climb with good cliff top views along the way. As with many places along this stretch of the coastline, the cliffs are unstable, so keep away from the edges both at the top and below.

Best Time of Year/Day

Sunset shots are possible from the end of September to the beginning of April and best between the end of October and the end of January. For sunrises visit between the end of November and the end of January.

Shots are possible at both high and low tide but be careful at high tide not to get cut off if you are shooting from the western end of the beach, or that the water level doesn't force you to set up near the base of the cliffs, as there is always the risk of a landslip.

Minimalist take on Eype Mouth; waves wash around a rock at dusk Canon 5D Mk II, Zeiss 21mm f/2.8, ISO 100, 13 seconds at f/11, 0.6 hard grad

Looking west from where the River Eype flows into the sea.
Canon 5D Mk II, 17-40mm f/4L at 17mm, ISO 100, 6 seconds
at f/22, polariser, LEE 1.2 ND

A colourful winter sunset at Eype Mouth. Thorncombe Beacon is in
the top right corner of the frame. Canon 5D Mk II, 24-105mm at
35mm, ISO 100, 10 seconds at f/6, LEE 0.9 soft grad and 1.2 ND

Colmer's Hill is a great subject on a misty morning.
Canon 5D Mk III, 70-200mm at 98mm, ISO 100, 0.5 sec at f/8

⑪ Colmer's Hill

Colmer's Hill overlooks the village of Symondsbury, just off the A35 west of Bridport. It is the area's main landmark, being clearly visible from the main road and from Bridport. The hill has a distinctive conical shape and is topped by pine trees planted there during the First World War.

After the Viking invasions the hill was named Sigismund's Berg after the Viking chief Sigismund. The named changed over time to Symondsbury, by which the village is still known. Colmer's Hill acquired its current name in the nineteenth century after the Reverend John Colmer, who owned the land and was village rector from 1805-06.

Symondsbury was known for cider production and there were a number of orchards in the area in the 18th century; just a couple remain today. There was also a quarry here from which neighbouring Quarry Hill and Quarr Lane get heir names. The quarry has since been reclaimed by nature but the undulations in the hill make an interesting feature.

What To Shoot and Viewpoints

From the layby, walk north along Quarr Lane. Take the left fork and go through the gate onto Quarry Hill.

Viewpoint 1 – From the Bottom of Quarry Hill

Walk up a gentle slope past some waterworks and set up just below a copse. From here there are excellent views of the hill as it rises above the horizon beyond; a good option if the light is a little flat and does not lift the hill from its background. Longer focal lengths are preferred here as the foreground is a little untidy and best left out of the frame.

Viewpoint 2 – From the Top of Quarry Hill

Once you reach the waterworks turn left and follow the footpath up the side of the copse. At the top of the hill turn to the right and walk along the ridge until you get good sight of Colmer's Hill. There are many spots you can stop and shoot from here, with a variety of focal lengths. The overlapping hill tops in front of Colmer's Hill make good foreground interest. Tighter crops isolating the top of the hill also work well, especially on misty mornings.

VP3: A winter morning at Colmer's Hill. Canon 5D Mk III, 24-105 at 32mm, ISO 100, 1/8 sec at f/11, polariser, LEE 0.6 hard grad

Colmer's Hill on a spring morning, from the lower part of Quarry Hill (VP 1). Canon 5Ds, 70-300mm at 70mm, ISO 100, 1/40 sec at f/8.0

How To Get Here

Colmer's Hill is just off the A35, about 1 ¾ miles west of Bridport, just south west of the village of Symondsbury. From Bridport drive west along the A35 for about 2 ¼ miles. Just as you reach the top of the hill there is a lay-by on the right, by the entrance to Quarr Lane (signposted). Take care as this is a fast road and you will be turning right into the lay-by, just in front of a blind summit. Great care will also be needed getting back out onto the main road.

Parking Lat/Long: 50.731952, -2.799603
Parking Postcode: DT6 6AG
Parking OS Map grid ref: SY 436 927

Map: OS Explorer 116 (1:25 000) Lyme Regis and Bridport

Accessibility

The lower viewpoint on Quarry Hill is an easy walk of a few hundred metres up a gentle slope. To get to the top of the hill requires a moderate level of fitness, as does Viewpoint 4 from Eype Down. There is no wheelchair access.

Best Time of Year/Day

Colmer's Hill photographs well at sunrise from all the viewpoints, though for good side lighting to reveal the shapes in the foreground from Viewpoint 3, winter is best. Spring and autumn can be very dramatic with the hill top rising from low-lying mist. Summer sunset can work well from the top of Quarry Hill (viewpoints 2 and 3).

Viewpoint 3 – From the North Side of Quarry Hill

Continue walking north along the top of Quarry Hill. You will then see the undulations left by the quarrying. These make excellent foreground interest in a wider angle shot, especially with low side lighting to accentuating the form and texture of the landscape.

Viewpoint 4 – From Eype Down

From the layby cross the road and walk up the track opposite. Fork left onto the footpath and walk up the slope of Eype Down. There are various spots here where you can stop and shoot Colmer's Hill with longer focal lengths.

At 910 feet (277 metres) Pilsdon Pen is the second highest point in Dorset – it is topped by Lewesdon Hill at 915 feet (279 metres). Pilsdon Pen is the site of an iron-age hill fort but there is evidence of occupation which pre-dates the hillfort; flint tools over 10,000 years old and Bronze Age burial mounds have been found. It was abandoned after the Roman conquest and has since only been used for grazing.

Pilsdon Pen has some of the best views in Dorset. Over the Marshwood Vale to the south, as far as the coast and Golden Cap, to the Axe Valley in the north and, on a good day, you can see as far as Exmoor and the Quantocks to the west. To the east, it is possible to see the Hardy Monument.

The land is owned by the National Trust but until 1982 it belonged to the Pinney family. In the late eighteenth century Dorothy and William Wordsworth rented a house near Pilsdon Pen from the Pinneys and spent much of their time walking in the local hills, including around Pilsdon Pen.

What To Shoot and Viewpoints

It is a stiff climb up the hill from the lay-by opposite the footpath, but worth the effort. Once at the top spend a few minutes orientating yourself. There are great views all around and the direction you shoot in will depend on the conditions. Is there an interesting sky? Is there mist in one of the valleys? Are there any wild flowers for foreground interest? Longer focal lengths are generally preferred from up here but there are also opportunities for wide angle compositions.

Viewpoint 1 – The Marshwood Vale

From the southern side of the hill top there are views south west over the Marshwood Vale. Focal lengths from 50mm upwards work well; look for patterns in the

patchwork of fields and the undulations of the hills. Hill tops and lone trees can be used as focal points in key parts of the frame.

Viewpoint 2 – Towards the Coast

Moving the camera around slightly to point south there is a view to the coast, which can include Colmer's Hill and Golden Cap. Focal lengths of 100mm or longer will generally work best for this view and again, you will need to try to find some sort of structure in the jumble of fields which lead into the distance.

Viewpoint 3 – Towards the East

From the eastern side of the hill you can compose over the ramparts towards sunrise. In late summer patches of heather can be used for foreground interest in wider angle shots.

Viewpoint 4 – Towards the North

Walk across to the northern end of the hillfort where there are far-reaching views over the Axe valley.

How To Get Here

Pilsdon Pen is 4 miles west of Beaminster in West Dorset and about 18 miles north west of Dorchester. From Dorchester take the A37 west and when just past Grimstone turn left onto the A356. After about 9 miles turn left onto the B3163, through Beaminster towards Broadwindsor. In Broadwindsor turn left just past the White Lion into West Street, the B3164. Stay on this road for just under 2 miles and just past Pilsdon Lane there is a lay-by on the left and the footpath up Pilsdon Pen is opposite this.

Parking Lat/Long: 50.804759, -2.833220
Parking Postcode: DT6 5NX
Parking OS Map grid ref: ST 413 009

Map: OS Explorer 116 (1:25 000) Lyme Regis and Bridport

Accessibility

It's a short but steep walk from the lay-by up to the top of Pilsdon Pen, something to consider if you're carrying long zooms, as recommended for many of the compositions. There is no disabled access.

Best Time of Year/Day

Because it is possible to shoot in all directions this is a location you can visit at any time of year and almost any time of day in the right conditions. Early mornings in spring and autumn will probably be favourite because of the possibility of low-lying mist and the distant hills emerging above it.

Looking south west across the Marshwood Vale before sunrise. Canon 1Ds Mk II, 24-105mm at 50mm, ISO 100, 45 sec at f/16, LEE 0.6 hard grad

The view towards the coast from Pilsdon Pen with Colmer's Hill in the distance. Canon 1Ds Mk II, 70-200mm at 145mm, ISO 100, 1/20 second at f/11, LEE 0.6 hard grad

Summer sunrise over Pilsdon Pen with heather and gorse in the foreground. Canon 5D Mk II, 17-40 at 17mm, ISO 100, 1.6 seconds at f/16, LEE 0.9 hard grad

The village of Charmouth lies at the mouth of the River Char overlooking Lyme Bay. The coast here is dominated by Golden Cap which, at 191 metres, is the highest sea cliff on the south coast of England. This stretch of coastline is popular with fossil hunters, especially after a landslip has created the possibility of new finds. The Charmouth Heritage Coast Centre acts as a visitor centre for the Jurassic Coast and has exhibitions and talks on the fossils found in the area. There is a fossil shop by the beach and also one in the village.

Golden Cap is owned by the National Trust and is visible for miles along the coastline. it takes its name from the outcrop of golden greensand rock at the top of the cliff. You can walk up from Charmouth, along the South West Coast Path, but the quicker way up is from the car park at Landgdon Hill.

What To Shoot and Viewpoints

Viewpoint 1 – Golden Cap from Charmouth Beach

From the car park furthest from the beach, cross the bridge over the river and walk onto the beach. From this side of the Char there are excellent views along the shore towards Golden Cap. You can simply compose following the shoreline or take a low viewpoint and use the waves washing over the pebbles as foreground interest.

There are also fantastic views inland from Golden Cap, looking over classic Dorset countryside. Canon 5Ds, 16-35mm f/4L at 32mm, ISO 100, 1/13 second at f/16, polariser. August

Viewpoint 2 – Sunrise from Charmouth Beach

The sun rises over the sea in winter and it is possible to shoot across the mouth of the river towards the sunrise, including Golden Cap in the composition.

Viewpoint 3 – From Golden Cap

You can get to Golden Cap by walking up the coast path from Seatown but the easier way to access it is from the National Trust car park – pay and display – free to members) at Langdon Hill, just outside Chideock. In the south east corner of the car park you will find the footpath to Golden Cap which, is well signposted. Follow this path through the woods and down the hill to a short, steep climb up to Golden Cap. From the top there are compositions in both directions along the coast. Along the cliff top, especially towards Seatown, you may find thrift in May. In late summer heather blooms on Golden Cap. Don't ignore the views inland; there is rolling Dorset countryside which can be photographed from here.

How To Get Here

Charmouth is about 20 miles west of Dorchester and a couple of miles east of Lyme Regis. From Dorchester, head west on the A35. Stay on the A35 past Bridport and through Chideock and Morecombelake. About 1.5 miles after Morcombelake turn left into The Street, signposted towards Charmouth. Drive past Newlands Holiday Park and follow the road into the village. Opposite the post office, turn left into Lower Sea Lane. There are two pay and display car parks at the end of the road.

To get to the Langdon Hill car park from Dorchester, take the first left past Chideock, then the next left and follow the signs to the Langdon Hill car park .

Charmouth Parking Lat/Long: 50.733549, -2.901216
Parking Postcode: DT6 6QX
Parking OS Map grid ref: SY 364 930

Langdon Hill Parking Lat/Long: 50.734696, -2.8340918
Parking Postcode: DT6 6SF
Parking OS Map grid ref: SY 412 931

Map: OS Explorer 116 (1:25 000) Lyme Regis and Bridport

Accessibility

It is an easy, level walk to get to the beach from the car park at Charmouth. There is no wheelchair access but some shots are possible by the Heritage Coast Centre, which is accessible for wheelchair users. The walk from Langdon Hill to Golden Cap requires a moderate level of fitness. There is no wheelchair access.

Best Time of Year/Day

Sunset shots from the beach are possible from mid-October through till March and sunrise shots are best between early November and early February, though the closer you are to midwinter the better.

Opposite: Late summer sunset from Golden Cap. Canon 5Ds, 16-35 at 24mm, ISO 100, 1/15 second at f/11, LEE 0.9 medium grad

The regency resort of Lyme Regis is a pretty enough town in its own right but is best known for the Cobb, its artificial harbour, built around 1250. Following its construction Lyme developed as a town and port but declined somewhat in the 1700s. The growing fashion for sea-bathing rescued it in the late 18th century and the town became a resort.

The Cobb is the main draw for photographers. In its original form it was constructed of oak piles with loose stones in between. Rebuilt in the 19th century, this time of Portland stone, the Cobb snakes out to sea forming the harbour and protecting the town from erosion. It's a great spot for leading lines and linear perspective, shooting east towards Golden Cap. It can be spectacular in stormy weather with waves crashing over it. It featured in the 1981 film The French Lieutenant's Woman.

What To Shoot and Viewpoints

Viewpoint 1 – East from the End of the Cobb

Walk out of the car park at its eastern end, past the lifeboat station and up onto the the Cobb. The harbour wall curves sharply left and you will see some buildings, including the aquarium, below. From just past this bend, with the aquarium to your left, you can shoot the Cobb as it curves round to the right leading the eye out along the coast towards Charmouth and Golden Cap. Camera height is important; too low and you won't have separation between the end of the the Cobb and the bottom of the cliffs in the distance. Take care here – the wall slopes down to the sea, which is where you will end up if you lose your footing. When the sea is rough waves crash over the Cobb with the potential to sweep you off.

Winter sunrise from the end of the Cobb. Canon 5D Mk II, Zeiss 21mm, ISO 100, 90 secs at f/11, LEE 0.6 hard grad, 1.2 ND

Viewpoint 2 – Looking West along the Cobb

For a slightly different take from the same spot, turn the other way and shoot towards the west. The wall curves to the right and you will see the cliffs of east Devon in the distance. This composition works well in portrait or a square aspect ratio and suits a monochrome conversion.

Viewpoint 3 – Along the Cobb

From further back the Cobb makes an 'S' shape. You can compose shots which include or exclude the buildings on the left – both are valid. This is a good, and safer option when the sea is rough.

Viewpoint 4 – The Harbour

The inner harbour makes a good subject, especially when the tide is high and it is full of fishing and pleasure boats. In summer the sun rises between the harbour walls.

Opposite: West from the Cobb. Canon 5D Mk II, 24-105mm at 24mm, ISO 100, 202 secs at f/11, B+W 10 stop ND, LEE 0.6 hard grad

How To Get Here

Lyme Regis is on the coast, just on the Dorset side of the border with Devon. From Dorchester drive west on the A35 for about 22 miles. Just past Charmouth take the second exit on the roundabout onto the A3052 and follow this into town. As you get into the town the roads are narrow and can get frustratingly congested at peak times. Continue through the town and up Pound Street. Towards the top of the hill turn left into Cobb Road, signposted Monmouth Beach. At the bottom of the hill turn right at the mini roundabout and you will see Monmouth Beach car park (pay and display) on your left.

Monmouth Beach Parking Lat/Long: 50.720136, -2.940562
Parking Postcode: DT7 3JN
Parking OS Map grid ref: SY 336 915

Map: OS Explorer 116 (1:25 000) Lyme Regis and Bridport

Accessibility

It is an easy, short and level walk to the Cobb from the car park. Disabled access is not possible onto the harbour wall but is possible on the promenade, where there are some alternative viewpoints. As detailed above, take great care when walking on the Cobb if the sea is rough as there is a very real danger of being washed off.

Best Time of Year/Day

Although the light can work well at either end of the day, the Cobb is a popular location that is best photographed at sunrise. You may need to negotiate your position with other photographers. Good shots are possible from mid-September to early March but the best results are when the sun is rising over the sea from late November to mid-January. For shots of the sun rising over the inner harbour, mid to late July is the ideal time.

Opposite: Summer sunrise over the inner harbour. Canon 5D, 17-40mm at 22mm, ISO 100, 1/15 second at f/6, LEE 0.9 hard grad

Although it is only a few minutes' drive from the A35, Eggardon Hill has an isolated, wild atmosphere, with panoramic views as far as the coast. The hill is an Iron Age hill fort dating back about 2,500 years but there are two Bronze Age burial mounds on the summit.

There is also smuggling history here. The notorious smuggler Isaac Gulliver, who owned Eggardon Hill Farm, planted a small clump of pine trees on the hill to act as a navigation guide for his ships as they approached the coast. The trees were later cut down but the earthworks built to protect them are still visible.

The southern half of the hill is owned by the National Trust and free public access is allowed year round. The northern half is privately owned and the hill is divided by a fence. A public footpath runs alongside the northern side of the fence, allowing access to one of the best viewpoints on the western side.

What To Shoot and Viewpoints

There are a couple of specific spots where it's worth setting up the tripod but one of the pleasures of this location is walking around and exploring – opportunities will present themselves as you do so.

Viewpoint 1 – The Ramparts

From the lay-by cross the road and walk north west along Kings Lane for a couple of hundred metres until you see a bridleway on the left. Follow the bridleway across the field to where it meets the entrance to the fort and other footpaths. From here you can walk around the ramparts, with excellent views to the south and west.

Looking south along the ramparts at sunset. Canon 1Ds Mk II, 17-40mm at 17mm, ISO 100, 1/10 second at f/16, LEE 0.9 hard grad

Viewpoint 2 – Bell Stone

As you follow the ramparts round to the north west corner, two fences meet. Climb over the stile and head west along the fence, following the footpath as marked on the OS map. After four or five hundred metres you will see an escarpment with some rocky ledges at the top – they are named 'Bell Stone' on the OS map. These ledges make excellent foregrounds for views towards the south east.

Viewpoint 3 – An Overview of the Fort

From the lay-by, cross the road and turn immediately left, rather than carrying on into Kings Lane. Follow the road south and then as it bends to the south west. There are superb views back towards the hill fort from here, especially towards the end of the day when low side-lighting emphasises relief on the ramparts. In misty or hazy conditions you can also get a layering effect with the hills receding into the distance. If you're feeling lazy you can drive along this road as there are several places where you can pull over briefly and set up your camera.

Opposite: Sheep grazing on the ramparts of the hill fort. Canon 1Ds Mk II, 24-105 f/4L at 60mm, ISO 100, 1 second at f/16, LEE 0.9 soft grad

How To Get Here

Eggardon Hill is approximately 9 ½ miles west of Dorchester. From Dorchester take the A35 west towards Bridport. Go through the village of Winterbourne Abbas and take the first right. At the end of the road turn left onto the old Roman Road. After about 3 miles you will reach a crossroads where you can see the hill fort to your left. There is a lay-by on the right with room for about three cars.

Parking Lat/Long: 50.748622, -2.6432794
Parking Postcode: DT2 0DS
Parking OS Map grid ref: SY 547 945

Map: OS Explorer 117 (1:25 000) Cerne Abbas and Bere Regis

Accessibility

This is a relatively easy location to access with no steep climbs, though it can be heavy underfoot at times. There is no wheelchair access.

Best Time of Year/Day

Eggardon suits the afternoon and evening. Viewpoints 1 and 3 work well pretty much all year round, and viewpoint 2 is best in the autumn and winter.

16 Hooke Park

Hooke Park is a woodland site owned by the Architectural Association, near the village of Hooke in West Dorset. The site is designated as ancient woodland and was originally a deer hunting estate. The college was established in 1983 by the Parnham Trust. The campus buildings are known for their experimental timber construction techniques.

The site is a 330-acre mixed woodland with beech, ash and conifers. The beech sections are particularly photogenic in the bluebell season – it is probably the best bluebell wood in the county. It is open to the public with footpaths giving access.

What To Shoot and Viewpoints

There are a couple of specific spots where it's worth setting up the tripod but one of the pleasures of this location is walking around and exploring opportunities as they present themselves.

Viewpoint 1

From the lay-by walk straight ahead onto the path. A little way along the path is a track to the right. If you take this track you can follow a circular walk which takes you back through the main entrance to Hooke Park and back onto the road where you can walk back to your car. Along the way there are various places where you can stop and photograph the bluebells, including sections of beech woodland with low leaves on some of the trees which catch the light nicely when the sun is low in the sky. To the left of the path the ground slopes gently upwards and is often a carpet of bluebells.

Viewpoint 2

If you continue past the path in Vewpoint 1 you will see some natural paths through the trees and bluebells. You can follow these into the woods to take you to the top of the slopes described in Vewpoint 1. The undulating ground in this part of the wood allows some interesting compositions.

Short telephoto focal lengths – around 70-100mm can work very well in bluebell woods as the compression effect can help to give the effect of a nice, thick carpet of bluebells. Polarisers will help to enhance colour saturation, not just of the bluebells, but all the foliage in the woodland.

Please stay on the footpaths and avoid trampling the bluebells.

A canopy of fresh, green leaves and sloping ground combine to make an interesting composition at Viewpoint 2.
Canon 5D Mk III, 24-105mm at 60mm, ISO 400, 2 seconds at f/16, polariser

Late afternoon sunlight catches the leaves above a carpet of bluebells at Viewpoint 1. Canon 5D Mk III, 70-200mm f/L at 98mm, ISO 400, 0.5 second at f/16, polariser

How To Get Here

Hooke Park is about 14 miles north west of Dorchester. From Dorchester head west on the A35 and take the third exit at the roundabout onto the A37. Take the first exit at the next roundabout to stay on the A37. Just past Grimstone turn left onto the A356, signposted to Crewkerne, Frampton and Maiden Newton. Stay on the A356 through the village of Frampton and the town of Maiden Newton. About 4.5 miles past Maiden Newton turn left onto Rampisham Hill, signposted towards Hooke and Powerstock. Take the left fork to stay on Rampisham Hill and in the village of Hooke turn right into Higher Street Lane. Follow Higher Street Lane as it bends round to the left and pass Hooke Court School on the right. At the end of the road turn left and you will see a small lay-by on your right. Here there is probably only enough room for one car. Alternatively you can turn right at the end of the road and on your left you will see the entrance to Hooke Park. It's possible to park here and then walk back up the road to Viewpoints 1 and 2, or follow the circular walk in the opposite direction to how it is described in Viewpoint 1.

Parking Lat/Long: 50.796803, -2.672747
Parking Postcode: DT8 3PB
Parking OS Map grid ref: SY 526 999

Map: OS Explorer 117 (1:25 000) Cerne Abbas and Bere Regis

Accessibility

The walks are mostly level and very easy through Hooke Park. Wheelchair access is possible along the track in Viewpoint 1 but not Viewpoint 2.

Best Time of Year/Day

Hooke Park really comes into its own during the bluebell season; bluebells peak at slightly different times each year but this is typically between the end of April and the middle of May. Good pictures can be had throughout the day but especially early morning and late afternoon / evening.

Looking across the Cerne towards Nether Cerne and its Norman church.
Canon 1Ds Mk II, 17-40 at 20mm, ISO 100, 1/4 second at f/16, polariser

Cerne Abbas is probably best known for the Giant – a 55 metre naked figure carved into the chalk hillside. It is thought by many to be an Iron Age fertility symbol, but its origins are uncertain as there are no records of it before the 18th century. The best views would be from a hot air balloon but with a long lens you can get good shots from the hill opposite.

Take a step back in time; the village is exceptionally pretty with some of the most beautiful 16th to 19th century buildings in Dorset. The Abbey was mostly destroyed in the Dissolution, though parts remain in the grounds of Abbey Farm such as the porch to the Abbot's Hall with its two-storey oriel window.

Nether Cerne and Up Cerne are easily accessed just off the main A352 and both have attractive flint and stone Norman churches set amongst the beautiful rural Dorset countryside.

What To Shoot and Viewpoints

Viewpoint 1 – The Abbots Porch, Cerne Abbas

Turn off the A352 into the village. Turn left past the New Inn into Abbey Street. Park considerately along here and you will find the entrance to the abbey grounds at the end – there is an honesty box for the entrance fee. Once inside you will see the Abbot's Porch ahead of you.

The Abbot's Porch in Cerne Abbas showing the oriel window.
Fuji X-Pro2, 10-24mm f/4 at 11mm, ISO 400, 1/800 second at f/11

Viewpoint 2 – Nether Cerne

Nether Cerne is just under 2 miles south of Cerne Abbas on the A352. There is a lay-by just before the village where you can park and shoot from the roadside. Take great care as it is a busy road. Alternatively, there is a turning into the hamlet itself. You can also walk to Nether Cerne along the footpath from Godmanstone. The best viewpoint for the church is from across the River Cerne.

Viewpoint 3 – Up Cerne

A mile or so north of Cerne Abbas is the hamlet of Up Cerne. There is a turning off the A352 into the hamlet but the best views of the church are probably from the roadside where you can show it nestled in the trees below the hills, with a small lake in front of it. Park in the lay-by just past the turning into the hamlet and walk south along the main road. Take care as this is a busy road. It is possible to climb onto the verge on the western side of the road and shoot through the hedgerows towards the church.

How To Get Here

Cerne Abbas is about 7 miles north west of Dorchester. From Dorchester head west on the A35, then at the Poundbury roundabout take the third exit onto the A37. Take the first exit at the next roundabout and then the first right onto the A352. After 6 miles turn right into the 'Folly' in Cerne Abbas. Nether Cerne is about 2 miles south of Cerne Abbas and Up Cerne a mile north.

Cerne Abbas Abbey Street Lat/Long: 50.810180, -2.476138
Postcode: DT2 7JQ
OS Map grid ref: ST 665 012

Lay-by for Nether Cerne Lat/Long: 50.780307, -2.472784
Postcode: DT2 7AQ
Parking OS Map grid ref: SY 667 979

Lay-by for Up Cerne Lat/Long: 50.825849, -2.480445
Parking Postcode: DT2 7AP
Parking OS Map grid ref: ST 662 030

Map: OS Explorer 117 (1:25 000) Cerne Abbas and Bere Regis

Accessibility

The key viewpoints in Cerne Abbas and Nether Cerne can be visited with very little walking involved. Wheelchair access is possible in the villages. If shooting Nether Cerne and Up Cerne from the roadside, you need to be careful as the A352 can be busy. The roadside views are not accessible for wheelchair users.

Best Time of Year/Day

The Abbey gardens look best with fresh foliage and spring flowers – there are lots of bluebells. Nether Cerne suits a winter afternoon with side-lighting on the church and fewer leaves on the trees to obstruct the view. Up Cerne works well on an autumn afternoon with colour in the trees.

Looking across the lake towards Up Cerne church on an autumn afternoon. Canon 1Ds Mk II, 24-105 at 105mm, ISO 100, 1/5 second at f/16, polariser

Cerne Abbas Giant shot through blossom in mid-April with a long lens from the opposite hillside. Canon 5D Mk III, 70-300 at 270mm, ISO 100, 1/80 second at f/14. © Stuart Holmes/fotoVUE

Another village on the River Cerne, Minterne Magna houses a hidden gem – Minterne Gardens. Minterne House has been owned by the Digby family for 350 years and the twenty acres of woodland garden were landscaped by Robert Digby in the style of Capability Brown. The general idea was that everything should look as natural as possible. While Capability Brown was working on the gardens at Sherborne Castle, Robert Digby would visit to pick his brains and try to implement the ideas in the gardens of Minterne House.

A series of small lakes and cascades were created by damming the stream running through the valley and trees were planted. Today there is a collection of Himalayan rhododendrons and azaleas along with many other plants and trees. The result is a very peaceful setting where it is possible to spend a lot time exploring the marked walks with your camera.

What To Shoot and Viewpoints

Rather than point out specific viewpoints the best thing to do is to spend some time following the walks through the gardens; you will find plenty to shoot, both in terms of general scenery and specific plants and flowers.

How To Get Here

Minterne Magna is 10 miles north of Dorchester and 9 miles south of Sherborne, on the A352. From Dorchester take the A37 towards Yeovil and then turn right onto the A352, Minterne Magna is 8 miles along the road. For the gardens there is a car park on the left, opposite the church. Cross the road to the entrance to the gardens. From Sherborne take the A352 towards Dorchester for 8 miles.

Parking Lat/Long: 50.837495, -2.485294
Parking Postcode: DT2 7AS
OS Map grid ref: ST 659 043

Map: OS Explorer 117 (1:25 000) Cerne Abbas and Bere Regis

Accessibility

The walk around the gardens is not strenuous and there are plenty of benches to sit down on, rest and enjoy the views. Most of walks are accessible for wheelchair users and are marked as such. There is an entry fee and you are restricted to visiting in opening hours: *www.minterne.co.uk/wp/opening-times*

Best Time of Year/Day

The gardens are usually open from mid-February to November 10am to 6pm, but check on the website for precise details.

Spring is an excellent time to visit for the blossom on the trees and the bluebells but the gardens also look good with autumn colour.

Opposite: Lady Eleanor's Bridge designed and built by Robert Digby in 1785, named after his wife. Fuji X-Pro2, 18-55mm at 38mm, ISO 400, 1/600 second at f/11

Bluebells and blossom on the garden walk. Fuji X-Pro2, 18-55mm f/2.8-4 at 55mm, ISO 400, 1/180 second at f/8.0

Great Dorset Steam Fair in August.
Fuji X-Pro2, 18-55mm at 18mm, ISO 800, 1/70 second at f/8.0

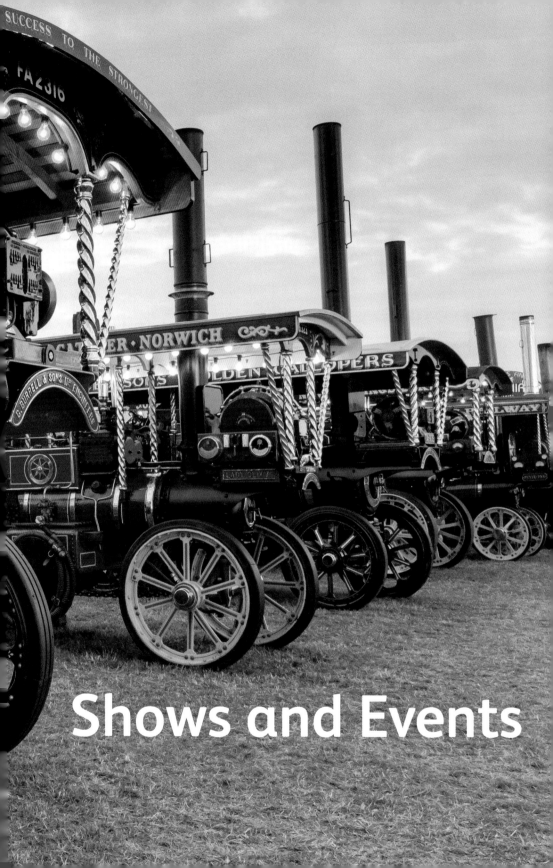

Shows and Events

Shows and Events

Dorset hosts a hugely diverse programme of outdoor shows and events that offer great opportunities for photography. There are carnivals, air shows, classic car and bike events, rural and agricultural shows, sailing regattas, the world's leading steam fair, a fossil festival, a hat festival and even knob throwing.

Some quick tips for photographing at shows.

- Check the event programme to see what is happening when and get there early or you may be fighting to get a good viewpoint.

- Keep in mind where the sun will be; it may be better to have your subject directly lit rather than photograph into the sun.

- Use longer focal lengths to get in close to the action or subject.

- Isolate the subject by using a wide aperture and narrow depth of field.

- Use the Auto or 'P' Program setting for grab shots – better to get the shot than miss it whilst fiddling with settings.

- Set the scene; look for compositions or subjects that identify the event.

- Don't forget detail; look for colour, shapes and textures that epitomise the event. Get creative using a narrow depth of field to isolate and emphasise the subject.

- Look for unusual viewpoints, get high or low to get something different than eye level.

- Photography in public places is allowed under UK law. Always ask permission if you want to take close ups of a person. There may be restrictions for photography if you are on private land or at a private event. For commercial use you will need a model release from the person you have photographed, or a property release if on private land.

Opposite: Fireworks over Swanage Bay during Carnival Week.
Canon 5Ds, 24-70mm f/4L at 66mm, ISO 100, 6.8 seconds at f/14

Pirates put in an appearance during Swanage Carnival Week.
Canon 5Ds, 70-300mm at 188mm, ISO 800, 1/4000 second at f/8

Shows and Events

Shows and Events Calendar – a selection, check local Tourist Information for more

March

Weymouth's Pirate Event .... www.weareweymouth.co.uk

Prehistory Weekend, Cranborne .... www.ancienttechnologycentre.co.uk

Swanage Blues Festival .... www.swanage-blues.org

April

Spring Steam Gala, Swanage .... www.swanagerailway.co.uk/events

Classic Cars on the Prom, Bournemouth .... www.classiccarsontheprom.com

St George's Day Festival – Poole .... www.pooletourism.com/events

Forde Abbey Tulip Festival .... www.fordeabbey.co.uk

Lyme Regis Fossil Festival .... www.fossilfestival.co.uk

May

Dorset Knob Throwing & Frome Valley Festival .... www.dorsetknobthrowing.com

Poole Maritime Festival .... www.poolemaritimefestival.uk

Weymouth Trawler Race

Poole Regatta .... www.pooleregatta.co.uk

Bournemouth Wheels Festival .... www.bournemouthwheels.co.uk

Sherborne Castle Country Fair .... www.sherbornecountryfair.com

June

Shaftsebury Festival .... www.shaftesburyfestival.co.uk

Corfe Summer Fair .... www.corfesummerfete.co.uk

Swanage Fish Festival .... www.swanagefishfest.org

Evershot Country Fair .... www.evershot.org/ecf

Larmer Tree Festival .... www.larmertreefestival.co.uk

Tankfest, Bovington .... www.tankmuseum.org/home

Folk on the Quay – Poole .... www.folkonthequay.co.uk

July

Chickerell Steam and Vintage Show .... www.chickerellsteamshow.uk

Camp Bestival, Lulworth Castle .... www.campbestival.net

Swanage Jazz Festival .... www.swanagejazz.org

Tolpuddle Martyr's Festival .... www.tolpuddlemartyrs.org.uk/festival

Leigh Food Fair and Vintage/Classic Car Show .... www.leighvillage.org.uk/foodfair

Swanage Carnival and Regatta .... www.swanagecarnival.com

Spirit of Portland Festival .... www.portlandcommunitypartnership.co.uk

Purbeck Valley Folk Festival .... www.purbeckfolk.co.uk

Shows and Events Calendar

August

Melplash Agricultural Show	www.melplashshow.co.uk
The Gillingham & Shaftesbury Show	www.gillshaftshow.co.uk
Weymouth Carnival	www.weymouthcarnival.co.uk
The Great Dorset Steam Fair, Tarrant Hinton	www.gdsf.co.uk
Nothe Fort Victorian Weekend, Weymouth	www.nothefort.org.uk
Bournemouth Air Festival	www.bournemouthair.co.uk
Purbeck Valley Folk Festival, near Corfe	www.purbeckfolk.co.uk
End of the Road Festival	www.endoftheroadfestival.com

September

Lyme Folk Weekend	www.lymefolk.com
Weymouth Regatta	www.weymouthregatta.uk
Weymouth Waterfest	www.weareweymouth.co.uk
Swanage Folk Festival	www.swanagefolkfestival.com
Bridport Hat Festival	www.bridporthatfest.org
Dorset County Show, Dorchester	www.dorsetcountyshow.co.uk

October

Gillingham Carnival	www.gillinghamcarnival.org.uk
Weymouth Lions Beach Motocross	www.weymouthlionsclub.co.uk
Swanage Blues Festival	www.swanage-blues.org

A pirate ship sailing into Swanage Bay for the start of Carnival Week.
Fuji X-Pro2, 18-55mm at 23mm, ISO 800, 1/3000 sec at f/8

Holy Trinity Church at West Lulworth, June evening.
Canon 1Ds Mk II, 17-40mm f/4L at 19mm, ISO 100, 1/6 second at f/16, LEE 0.6 soft grad, polariser.

Dorset Villages

Dorset Villages

Dorset's villages are some of the prettiest in the country. There are many thatched cottages, some made from cob, a natural building material consisting of subsoil, water, straw and lime. Some villages feature stone cottages built from Purbeck stone or the warmer-coloured Ham stone. Many have their roots back in the 10th century. There are picturesque churches, some dating back to the 12th century.

Abbotsbury (page 188) has stone cottages, a tithe barn, the Swannery and is close to Chesil Beach and St Catherine's Chapel.

Corfe Castle (page 34), better known for its castle, is a very beautiful village and interesting in its own right.

The 18th century 'model' village of **Milton Abbas,** featuring a row of white thatched cottages, was built by Joseph Damer (later Lord Milton) to replace the village he demolished as it was too close to his mansion.

Cerne Abbas (page 216) is famous for its Giant – a chalk carving in the nearby hills but the village is very pretty and often surprisingly quiet.

For many people **West Lulworth** (page 86) is simply where you park your car when visiting **Lulworth Cove** or **Durdle Door**, but the village itself is worth looking around. Best visited out of season, here you will enjoy a quintessentially English village.

Worth Matravers is one of Purbeck's most beautiful stone villages. In the centre is a small green and an attractive, well-kept duckpond. From here you can walk to **Winspit** (page 62) and **Seacombe** (page 60) or pop into the Worth Matravers Tea and Supper Room for some of the best food in the area. The atmospheric Square and Compass pub is popular with locals and is famous for its range of ciders and its pasties.

If you're on a shoot at **Knowlton Church** (page 128), then you could also pop down the road to the village of **Wimborne St Giles**. Here there is a row of beautiful almshouses and the church of St Giles is very photogenic.

The River Tarrant is a tributary of the Stour and there are a number of villages in the Tarrant valley, including **Tarrant Hinton** which hosts the Great Dorset Steam Fair. My personal favourite is **Tarrant Monkton** with its cob and thatched cottages and a ford through the river. For refreshments, the Langton Arms, a 17th century inn, won't disappoint.

Close to Dorchester is **Sydling St Nicholas**, a beautifully preserved picturesque village with stone and flint thatched cottages and many small bridges over Sydling Water. Also near Dorchester is **Stinsford** with its Thomas Hardy associations; the author loved the church and it's where his heart is buried, in the grave of his first wife. There are also some very pretty riverside walks nearby.

Tolpuddle, located between Bere Regis and Dorchester is a name very familiar to students of British history. It is famous for the Tolpuddle Martyrs – six farm labourers who were transported to Australia in 1834 for attempting to set up an agricultural trade union. They were pardoned some four years later. There is a museum and every year the Tolpuddle Martyrs Festival is held here.

There are many others worth visiting. Those listed below are some of my personal favourites; this is, of course, entirely subjective and I hope I don't cause offence if I've missed out your favourite village.

Quirky Names

Dorset has its fair share of odd and amusing place names. The Piddle Valley causes some mirth and here you will find the villages of Piddlehinton and Piddletrenthide. Whitchurch Canonicorum, Ryme Intrinseca and Toller Porcorum all sound very grand, and one of the most photographed village signs in the UK must be that of Shitterton near Bere Regis.

List of Villages	Parking Lat/Long	Postcode	OS Maps Co-ordinates
Abbotsbury	50.665116, -2.597554	DT3 4JL	SY 578 852
Cerne Abbas	50.811788, -2.479024	DT2 7GY	ST 663 014
Corfe Castle	50.642002, -2.059093	BH20 5DR	SY 959 824
Milton Abbas	50.816668, -2.273545	DT11 0BP	ST 808 019
Stinsford	50.718628, -2.410080	DT2 8XW	SY 711 910
Sydling St Nicholas	50.795349, -2.523426	DT2 9PD	SY 632 996
Tarrant Monkton	50.879127, -2.080808	DT11 8RX	ST 944 088
Tolpuddle	50.749413, -2.295357	DT2 7EW	SY 792 944
West Lulworth	50.620018, -2.253482	BH20 5RQ	SY 821 800
Wimborne St Giles	50.907436, -1.956742	BH21 5LZ	SU 031 119
Worth Matravers	50.598717, -2.037935	BH19 3LE	SY 974 776

Thatched cottage at Tarrant Monkton, winter morning.
Canon 1Ds Mk II, 17-40 at 17mm, ISO 200, 1/80 sec at f/9.0, polariser

Spring shower over St Oswald's Bay.
Canon 5Ds; 16-35mm f/4L at 22mm, ISO 200, 8 seconds at f/11, LEE 4-stop ND, polariser

Photographing the
Jurassic Coast

Photographing the Jurassic Coast

The Dorset coastline has always attracted visitors but its appeal increased significantly in 2001 when a 96 mile (154 km) stretch of south coast was designated a World Heritage Site.

The so-named *Jurassic Coast* extends from Old Harry Rocks near Studland to Orcombe Point near Exmouth in Devon. The Dorset section includes a variety of landscape types from high precipitous cliffs to sandy beaches, rocky coves and harbours to fishing villages, as well as textbook geology locations such as Lulworth Cove and Durdle Door.

But you don't have to be a student of geology to appreciate the beauty here; for photographers there is a wealth of subject matter.

Planning

Research and planning are key when shooting the coast. A lot can be done prior to visiting a location, using this book and online resources such as Google and Flickr, or the stock libraries will give you a feel for what to expect from a location and provide inspiration for compositions. There is no substitute however for visiting a location and scouting it for yourself. Check it out in the middle of the day and work out what tide height is likely to suit it best and where the light will fall at different times of day. The sun compass at the front of this book is a useful tool and there are also apps such as the Photographer's Ephemeris or Sunscout, which use augmented reality to show the sun position at different times of day and year.

Keep an open mind

Where possible try to make your own decisions about what might suit a location. Be opportunistic and make the most of prevailing conditions. It's easy to be influenced by received wisdom but this can blind us to other opportunities. Some photographers will tell you, for example, that Kimmeridge Bay needs to be photographed at low tide and the angle of the sun is best in winter. The reality is there are excellent high tide options and from the right viewpoints, midsummer works as well as any other time of year.

Weather Watching

Don't forget to check the weather forecast and plan accordingly. There is no ideal weather for coastal landscapes – overcast conditions can be perfect for long exposure photography, stormy weather can produce dramatic light and few photographers can resist a colourful sunset. Perhaps the hardest conditions are when there are plain, blue skies without a cloud to be seen – but even then, with the right approach (leaving the sky out of the frame, concentrating on details, etc.) you can produce successful images.

Wind and Spray

Pay attention to wind speed which can be an issue both for clifftop and shoreline photography. On the shore if the wind is blowing in from the sea at speeds much in excess of 15mph (24kph), this can result in sea spray coating your camera and lens or filters. As well as being potentially harmful to your equipment, it will coat your lens with salt, reducing image quality. Keep an eye on the front element of your lens or filters if you are using them and clean them when the spray begins to build up. A lens cloth alone will not be much help – this will just spread the spray around, rather than remove it – so a good lens cleaning fluid, such as that produced by Zeiss, is recommended. Beyond a certain point however, there will be too much spray to cope with and you should look for alternatives to shoreline compositions.

On clifftops wind can cause problems by blowing foliage and causing it to blur. If you are planning on shooting clifftop flowers, conditions need to be almost completely still to prevent movement. Increasing the ISO will allow for faster shutter speeds to freeze movement but at the cost of reduced image quality.

A colourful sunrise over St Oswald's Bay.
Canon 5D Mk II, Zeiss 21mm, ISO 100, 60 seconds at f/16, LEE 4-stop ND, 0.9 soft grad

Equipment for Shooting Seascapes

The following equipment is recommended:

- **Lenses:** wide angle zoom (16-35mm), standard zoom (24-70mm), telephoto zoom (70-200mm).

- **Tripod:** The sturdier the better.

- **Filters (optional):** a set of neutral density graduated filters, ranging from 1–3 stops, hard and soft-edged, a set of 'full' neutral density filters, perhaps a 4-stop, 6-stop and 10-stop.

- **Remote Cable:** to avoid camera shake when firing the shutter and also to allow long exposure photography (in excess of 30 seconds) via the camera's BULB (B) setting.

- **Cleaning Cloth and Fluid:** necessary for wiping off sea spray and splashes of water on the lens.

- **Rain Cover:** can be used to protect your camera from being soaked by rogue waves or sea spray.

- **Batteries:** take enough fully-charged batteries for a day's shooting. Remember that long exposures and using live view will drain batteries faster than 'normal' use.

- **Head Torch:** Very useful for dawn and dusk shoots.

Tide and Weather Apps and Websites

- **Tides Planner**: *www.imray.com/tides-planner-app*

- **AyeTides App**: *www.ayetides.com*

- **Sunscout**: uses your phone's camera and augmented reality to show the position of the sun.

- *www.metoffice.gov.uk*: the met office gets a bit of an unfair reputation for inaccuracy. If you use the local forecasts, rather than look at the broader regions, they are very accurate, especially once you get to within 48 hours.

- *www.metcheck.com*

- **The Photographer's Ephemeris**: sunrise and sunset times and angles for any location in the world at any time, plus much more useful information.

- **PhotoPills**: includes a sunrise / sunset planner, overlaid on maps or with augmented reality, plus golden hour, blue hour times and much more.

Opposite page left: A marker post on Swanage beach makes an excellent minimalist study. Canon 5D Mk III, 24-105mm at 82mm, 8 secs at f/16, LEE 3-stop ND

Opposite page right: Dusk at Worbarrow Bay, looking towards Mupe Rocks. Canon 1Ds Mk II, 24-105mm f/4L at 28mm, ISO 100, 121 seconds at f/11, LEE 4-stop ND, LEE 0.9 soft grad

Coastal Cliff Tops

Clifftop viewpoints can give breathtaking views along the coast providing an enhanced feeling of scale and context. For these higher viewpoints you will find both wide angle and telephoto lenses useful.

If positioned above a drop, looking down with a wide angle lens can exaggerate the height of the cliff. You can also use a wide angle lens to place emphasis on foreground elements such as rocks, footpaths and wild flowers, which not only provides a lead-in to the composition but also creates depth and perspective.

Telephoto lenses can be used to create layered compositions, as they reduce the apparent distance between headlands thus creating a stacking effect. This can be enhanced by side lighting, atmospheric haze or sea spray in the air.

Telephotos are also useful on stormy days, allowing you to focus attention on fierce waves crashing over rocks below. When shooting these kind of scenes you can freeze the action with a shutter speed of around 1/250 second or use a neutral density filter to slow the movement down, capturing the wave motion as swirling, white trails with an exposure of several seconds.

Good clifftop views are possible in Dorset throughout the year though along the majority of the coastline the sun is at its best angle between early October and mid-March. May, June and July are also good months, as this is when wild flowers bloom on the clifftops.

Best Cliff-top Locations

- Handfast Point / Old Harry Rocks (page 48)
- St Aldhelm's Head & Emmett's Hill (page 64)
- Durdle Door (page 90)
- Mupe Bay (page 82)
- Golden cap (page 206)

Tip

When shooting at sunrise and sunset it's always tempting to shoot towards the colour but directional light works extremely well with clifftop views, revealing texture and adding contrast and depth. Don't forget to look for compositions which exploit this.

Summer sunrise at Old Harry Rocks. Fuji X-Pro2, 10-24mm at 10mm, ISO 200, 15 secs at f/16, LEE 4-stop ND, LEE 0.6 medium grad

Opposite: Durdle Door from the cliff path on a spring evening. Fuji X-Pro2, 10-24mm f/4 at 12mm, ISO 400, 1/25 second at f/14

Shoreline Views

The shoreline lets you get close to the action. Try capturing waves crashing over rocks or washing up over the shore. Look for rock pool reflections, jagged rocks and smooth boulders for foreground, smooth sand with wave patterns, tidal pools and reflected colour. Wide views are the obvious choice on beaches, but more intimate, miniature landscapes also work extremely well.

When shooting at sea level, the scene can change dramatically over a short time period compared to the general views you get from the cliff tops. Storms can radically change the shape and size of beaches, adding new material or removing sand and shingle.

Tide height, time of day and year as well as the state of the sea will all play a huge part in compositions here; everything being much more immediate.

Wide sandy beaches lend themselves to simplicity; paring down compositions to their essential elements is often the way to go. Look for reflections in wet sand and pebbles, boulders or ripples in the sand for foreground interest, whilst structural elements such as groynes and marker posts can act as lead-in lines or focal points. Minimalist compositions made up of simple

Mupe rocks, pre-dawn. Nikon D800, 16-35mm f/4 at 20mm, ISO 100, 20 seconds at f/16, LEE 4-stop ND, LEE 0.6 hard grad

bands of sand, sea and sky can work well on beaches, especially with long exposures to smooth out the sea and blur the boundaries between water and land.

Sandy beaches generally look their best on a falling tide; as the water recedes, the sand is left wet, clean and free of footprints. Early or late in the day (depending on the orientation of the beach and time of year) are generally better as there will be fewer people around. One or two people can enhance a wide beach view – a lonely figure on a deserted beach adds an air of romance and mystery.

For a sunset shoot arrive in plenty of time – up to two hours before the sunset – in order to make the most of the golden light in the hour or so before the sun sets. Similarly, when shooting the sunrise, don't pack up the moment the sun breaks the horizon; beaches can look their best with low, warm light enhancing the golden colour of the sand and revealing its texture.

Rocky beaches and bays can appear cluttered and confusing to the eye. The trick is to shoot them when the tide is at the right height – low enough to reveal some interesting features, but high enough to hide any distractions. Scouting locations and working this out using tide tables is crucial.

Falling tides are easier to work with – you're less likely to find yourself retreating up the beach and getting wet feet, or worse, if you misjudge the size of an incoming wave.

Shooting the backwash of waves can create dynamic trails leading out to sea, espcially if there are rocks around which the water can swirl. The ideal shutter speed depends on the size and speed of the waves but usually between one and three seconds gives good results. Longer than this and the waves will often blur too much, losing shape and texture.

If you use extreme neutral density filters, such as the LEE Big Stopper, for long exposures, give the moving elements of the scene plenty of space – a more minimalist approach will generally give better results.

Kimmeridge Bay at high tide in mid-summer. Fuji X-Pro2, 10-24 at 13mm, ISO 200, 6 secs at f/11, LEE 6-stop ND, LEE 0.6 med grad

Look for something to contrast with the moving elements. Dark, jagged rocks for example contrast well with soft, white water.

Best Sandy or Shingle Beaches

Best Rocky Bays

Tip

Getting sharp results can be tricky when shooting on beaches, especially sandy ones, as not only can your tripod be knocked by waves during the exposure, but the tripod can sink in the sand. Try pushing your tripod legs firmly into the sand before you begin your exposure.

Coastal Architecture and Structures

The coast has its own unique architecture and structures: lighthouses, piers, harbour walls and groynes. These make effective lead-ins and focal points in wider compositions as well as excellent subjects in themselves. If you like bold, graphic compositions or more structured images will love the potential offered by locations such as the Victorian pier in Swanage (page 50).

Shooting coastal architecture has potential for allowing you to contrast natural and man-made elements and for

Portland Bill long exposure minimalism. Canon 5D Mk II, 17-40 f/4L at 21mm, ISO 100, 180 secs at f/22, 10-stop ND, 0.9 soft grad

illustrating the power of nature. Huge waves crashing down on piers or lighthouses are classic compositions. Dorset doesn't tend to get the same big storms as Cornwall's Atlantic coast but they do occur once in a while so make the most of them when they happen. Safety is paramount; keep well away from cliff edges and maintain a safe distance from the waves; shooting from further back with a long lens is definitely recommended when the sea is rough.

Coastal structures are a very good option when the weather is dull, especially if there is some texture in the sky. This is the time to get out your neutral density filters and try long exposures of piers, lighthouses and breakwaters. Keep compositions as clean as possible and allow plenty of space around the subject so that the moving elements contrast effectively with it. Black and white conversions of these types of shot are always worth trying.

Piers

Lighthouses

Harbour Walls

Swanage Old Pier long exposure on a dull day. Canon 5D Mk II, 17-40 at 21mm, ISO 100, 304 secs at f/16, 10-stop ND, 0.9 soft grad

Coping with Contrast

One of the main technical problems encountered in landscape photography is that very often the sky is much brighter than the foreground. The human eye is very good at distinguishing detail in both the deep shadows and bright highlights, but cameras are not yet able to do so. If the dynamic range – the difference between the brightest highlights and the darkest shadows – of the scene exceeds the dynamic range of the camera's sensor, then either the highlights *blow* so that they become pure white with no detail, or the shadows *block up* so that they become pure black.

Whilst the latest camera sensors are improving, they still have some way to go. To recreate what the eye can see you will need to compress the tonal range of the scene either by using in-camera filtration or by blending a series of bracketed exposures.

Graduated Filters

The in-camera solution is to use a neutral density graduated filter ('ND grad' or 'grad' for short). These filters have a neutral grey top half and a clear bottom half with a transition zone in the middle. The method is to place the dark half over the bright sky and you bring the tonal range of the scene within the sensor's dynamic range. In order to cope with different lighting conditions and varying topography, they come in different strengths – typically, one, two or three stops – and also with soft or hard transition zones. Soft grads have a more gentle transition which is useful when the horizon is uneven or interrupted. LEE Filters have introduced a range of medium grads with a transition zone somewhere between hard and soft and a set of grads with a 'very hard' transition zone.

Filter systems

There are two types of filter – the screw-in type which screws directly onto the front of your lens and system filters which slot into a dedicated filter holder attached to the lens. As the latter allow you to move the filter up and down in the holder and give you complete control over where you place the transition zone, they are the better option. Popular makes include LEE, Cokin and Formatt-Hitech.

Method

The key to using grads is choosing the right strength and lining them up correctly with the horizon line so that their use is not obvious. Generally speaking, hard grads should be used with horizons which are mostly level and soft (or medium) grads with uneven horizons which are broken by features such as hills or buildings. Choosing the correct strength grad becomes easier with experience though it's always worth checking the review image to make sure that the full tonal range is captured and that you haven't *overgradded* and made the sky unnaturally dark – a common error.

Taking meter readings from the darker foreground and brighter parts of the sky and calculating the difference in brightness can help the selection process. When choosing your filter, remember the aim is not to remove the difference in brightness between foreground and sky, but to reduce it. For a sky to look natural it should be lighter than the land or water.

Positioning grads well requires practice. Some find it easier to use the viewfinder and others prefer to do this using the live view screen on the back of the camera. With an optical viewfinder, one useful trick is to engage the depth of field preview, which will darken the viewfinder and can make it easier to spot the transition line. I find that gently wiggling the filter up and down in the holder helps to identify where the transition is.

Check the review screen to ensure correct placement of the filter – inexperienced users tend to place the filter too low in the frame, so that it 'cuts into' the foreground.

Winter sunset from Peveril Point, Swanage. Canon 5D, 17-40mm f/4L at 21mm, ISO 100, 4 seconds at f/14, 0.9 hard grad

Even after the sun has set, the contrast is often too high for the scene to be captured without filtration. Poole Harbour, summer sunset. Pentax 67II, 45mm f/4, Fuji Velvia, LEE 0.9 soft grad

September sunrise, Hod Hill. Canon 5D Mk III, 24-70mm f/4L at 24mm, ISO 100, 1/30 second at f/11, LEE 0.9 hard grad

Exposure Blending

There are advantages to using graduated filters rather than a software solution for controlling contrast. Capturing the scene in a single frame makes it easier to review and assess on the camera's rear LCD and there is always the danger that elements in the scene can move between frames making exposure blending difficult. Worse, if the light changes significantly between exposures, as can happen with longer exposures, then getting a natural-looking blend becomes difficult.

However, there are occasions when filters just won't work. Sometimes the contrast is so great that even your darkest grad won't compress the tonal range enough and combining grads can be very tricky.

On occasions, a horizon line is so uneven, that it's impossible to position even a soft grad without its use becoming apparent. This is especially true when shooting on the shoreline with cliffs on one side of the image. In these situations the only solution is to take a series of shots at different exposures – known as bracketing – and then combine them in software to create a single image which contains the full brightness range of the scene.

Until recently the best way to get natural-looking results was to manually blend exposures using layer masks in Photoshop. However, the HDR functions in the latest versions of Adobe Lightroom and Camera Raw in Photoshop can give excellent results and are easy to use.

Follow this simple step-by-step tutorial to learn how to blend exposures in the latest versions of Lightroom.

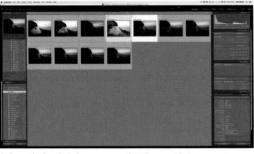

1. From the bracketed exposures, select the ones that you want to blend. You will need a minimum of 2 – one exposed for the highlights and one for the shadows, though additional shots between the extremes can give you more control.

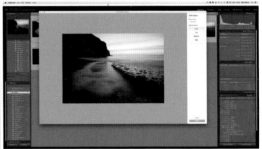

2. Go to Photo > Photomerge > HDR. Lightroom will create a preview image with various options. Check 'Autoalign' but experiment with 'Deghost Amount'; in this case, setting it to 'None' gave the most pleasing result. 'Auto Tone' rarely seems to give good results, so leave this unchecked so you can do the tone-mapping yourself. Click 'Merge'

3. Lightroom creates a dng raw file, which you can then open up in the Develop module and process as you would any other file, adjusting white balance, contrast, colour saturation and so on.

The final image shows a full range of tones, but still retains a natural look. This would not have been achievable with a single image. Dancing Ledge, November sunrise.

With an uneven horizon, it can be difficult to use graduated filters without the transition
line 'cutting in' to buildings, hills or trees. For this shot of Knowlton Church, two
exposures – one for the sky and for the foreground – were blended together.
Canon 5D Mk II, Zeiss 18mm f/3.5, ISO 100, f/11.

In bright sunlight with the LEE Super Stopper (15-stop ND) an exposure time of four minutes was achieved.
With a lower ISO and smaller aperture this could have been even longer. Kimmeridge Bay, October.
Canon 5Ds, 16-35mm at 27mm, ISO 200, 240 seconds at f/8, LEE Super Stopper, LEE 0.6 hard grad.

Long Exposures

Long Exposures

There are two main approaches to photographing water – use a fast shutter speed to freeze the movement or a slow shutter speed to blur it. Longer shutter speeds can elicit a Marmite response – viewers either love or hate it.

Personally, I love the way moving elements are recorded differently to how the eye perceives them; rippled water is rendered smooth and glassy with enhanced reflections, waves become a misty blur, and moving clouds brushstrokes. The overall effect creates an ethereal, romantic atmosphere. Dorset's Jurassic Coast is the perfect place to experiment with this technique.

Neutral Density Filters

Shooting a long exposure isn't just a matter of opening the shutter for as long as you want. If you do this in anything other than very low light – even with the lens stopped right down – you'll get a very overexposed picture.

Using neutral density (ND) filters – filters with a neutral grey coating which blocks the amount of light reaching the camera's sensor – gives photographers the ability to artificially extend exposure times but, until recently, were limited to 3 or 4 stops in density meaning creative effects were only really possible in relatively low light.

With the introduction of 'extreme' ND filters, such as the LEE Big Stopper (10 stops) and the LEE Super Stopper (15 stops), long exposures have become much easier to achieve, even in bright daylight. Long exposure photography has since boomed in popularity. To give an idea of how extreme these filters are, if you shoot an unfiltered exposure of 1/15 second, to get an equivalent exposure using a 10-stop filter will require an exposure time of 1 minute. With a 15-stop filter, you will need to open the shutter for 32 minutes.

Waves on the rocks at Burton Bradstock. Canon 5D Mk II, Zeiss 21mm, ISO 100, 30 seconds at f/11, LEE 4-stop ND & 0.9 soft grad

It's worth carrying a range of ND filters with you in order to deal with different lighting conditions – I usually have a 3-stop, 4-stop, 6-stop, 10-stop and 15-stop in my bag. If shooting towards the end of the day you will find that the extreme NDs generate unworkably long exposures and they are therefore probably best saved for brighter conditions in the middle of the day. My most-used filters are a 4-stop and 6-stop.

With less dense filters, such as the 4 and 6-stop, depending on the light, you can usually meter fairly accurately through the lens; focusing is also often possible, at least using live view, if not through the viewfinder of an SLR. With more extreme filters, metering becomes a problem (cameras will only meter accurately down to a certain EV level) and focusing through the viewfinder is also extremely difficult. You should therefore use the following procedure.

Long Exposure Shooting Technique

- Set up your camera on a tripod, without the ND filter, and attach a cable release.
- Compose your shot.
- Focus and then switch to manual focus so that the camera doesn't hunt when the ND is in place.
- Meter the scene and shoot.
- Review the shot and check the exposure using the histogram.
- Calculate the filtered exposure: double the exposure time for every stop. For example, if the unfiltered exposure is 1/30 second, to find the correct exposure with a 10-stop filter, double this 10 times, i.e. 1/15, 1/8, 1/4, 1/2…… 32 seconds. Some manufacturers supply an exposure conversion chart with their filters and there are also various smart phone apps available.
- Use Manual exposure mode for exposures of less than 30 seconds and Bulb mode for exposures of longer than 30 seconds, locking the shutter open for the required length of time.
- Review the image and check the exposure using the histogram. Sometimes even when your calculations are correct the exposure will be out. Lighting conditions can change while the shutter is open, making your calculations invalid. Sometimes the actual density of your filter may not be exactly as indicated, especially so with extreme NDs.
- If necessary, adjust exposure and re-shoot. When you are dealing with long exposures you need to make big adjustments if your exposure is wrong. For example, increasing a 2-minute exposure by just half a stop makes it 3 minutes.

A two-minute exposure at Swanage. Canon 5D Mk II, Zeiss 21mm f/2.8, ISO 100, 122 seconds at f/22, B+W 10-stop ND, LEE 0.6

Rules are useful but it's important to know when to break them. With no interest in the sky, a two-thirds/one third division wouldn't have been so effective. It was more important to place emphasis on the layers of fields and trees leading towards the background focal point. Marshwood Vale from Pilsdon Pen, late summer morning. Canon 5Ds, 70-300mm at 182mm, ISO 200, 1/20th second at f/11

Composition

Composition in Landscape Photography

Good landscape photography depends on a combination of the right subject or location, shooting in the right light and composition. Of these three, I would argue that good composition is the most important. It can be frustrating to view a well-composed shot of a great location in poor light, but it's far more frustrating to have a great location shot in stunning light but with a composition you know doesn't do it justice.

Composition is essentially a problem-solving activity. The problems are how to arrange the elements in the frame to create a sense of balance and harmony and how to create a sense of depth and perspective in a two-dimensional medium.

Organising the Frame

The main goal of composition is to find a sense of order and harmony in the chaos of the natural world. There are many ways of organising elements in the frame to achieve this.

Rule of Thirds at Mupe Rocks. The large sea stack sits precisely on the top right intersection. Canon 5Ds, 16-35mm f/4L at 16mm, ISO 200, 25 seconds at f/11, LEE Little Stopper

Rule of Thirds

Imagine a grid dividing the viewfinder into thirds, both horizontally and vertically, so that it looks like a noughts and crosses grid. You can then organise the elements in the frame around these divisions.

The obvious starting point is the horizon, which can be placed on one of the horizontal lines. Then move on to the other points of interest. Most images benefit from having a strong focal point in the frame and the intersections of the horizontal and vertical lines in the grid are particularly powerful places to position such a point of interest. Placing the main subject here rather than in the centre of the frame generally results in a more dynamic composition as the eye is encouraged to travel around the frame to find the subject.

The Rule of Thirds is derived from, and is a simplification of, a proportion known as the Golden Section. This should, in theory, provide an even more harmonious division of the frame. This proportion has been used in art and architecture for centuries and is also common in the natural world. Research suggests that our brains are 'hard-wired' to respond positively to images which conform to the Golden Section proportions.

Golden Section

To create a Golden Section, divide the image frame into two rectangles, so that the ratio of the smaller one to the larger one is the same as the ratio of the larger one to the whole frame. Expressed mathematically, this ratio is approximately 1:1.618. These sections can then be subdivided according to the same ratio so that you end up with a grid which looks a little like a 'squashed' Rule of Thirds grid. As with the Rule of Thirds grid, use it to help you with the placement of key elements; strong focal points can again be placed on the intersections of horizontal and vertical lines.

Golden Section. The pillars of rock in this shot are lined up with the Golden Section grid. Looking over Chapman's Pool from Emmett's Hill, late spring sunset. Fuji X-Pro2, 10-24mm f/4 at 14mm, ISO 200, 9 seconds at f/11, LEE 4-stop ND and 0.9 hard grad

Golden Spiral

Closely related to the Golden Section is the Golden Spiral. If you keep dividing the frame according to the Golden Ratio, then connect the opposite corners of the rectangles in the grid, the result is a Golden Spiral. As a compositional guide, the Golden Spiral is less easy to apply than Thirds or the Golden Section grid, but it is interesting to note how many successful images fit its pattern.

Visual Balance

Formal divisions of the frame, such as the Rule of Thirds and the Golden Section work well, but if we only ever follow these 'rules' our images will soon become formulaic and predictable. Worse, simply applying the principles blindly without any consideration, can result in poor compositions, so it's worth taking a little time to get to grips with the principles of visual balance.

In many ways visual balance is similar to physical balance and making this comparison can help us understand how it works. If you place two objects of equal weight on a seesaw, they need to be equidistant from the fulcrum to be balanced. In visual terms, we would have symmetry, which is often considered harmonious but somewhat static. If you have objects of different weights, the lighter one will have to be further away from the fulcrum in order to achieve balance, which in visual terms would create an asymmetric balance – usually considered to be more dynamic.

In reality, visual balance is more complex than this, but the basic principle is true. While we can't consider the physical weight of objects in the frame, we can consider the factors which contribute to their 'visual weight' – size, brightness, contrast, complexity, texture and so on – and place them in the frame accordingly.

Visual balance: There are two main points of interest which balance each other in this image – Corfe Castle and the rising sun.

Composition in Landscape Photography

Leading Lines

As well as placing the focal point of a landscape in a key part of the frame, it is also possible to emphasise it by careful use of lines to lead the eye through the frame. This can help to highlight the relationship between the subject and the foreground and enhance the feeling of depth in a photograph.

Lines are everywhere in the landscape from man-made roads, paths and hedgerows, to natural features such as rivers or the coastline. Lines also don't have to be 'real' but can be implied, such as the patterns created by waves or any row of objects.

Using implied lines is a subtle but effective way of highlighting the focal point in a landscape. It's not always easy to do, but if you can find a composition in which other objects are pointing towards the main subject, the result will be a more powerful composition. Wide angle lenses can help here, as the distortion present at the edges of the frame can stretch and enhance lines. Having 'pointers' in the corners of the frame helps direct attention inward and stop the eye wandering out of the frame.

Wide angle distortion has helped with the angles in this shot, the lines coming in from the corners act as 'pointers' to the main focal point in the background. Kimmeridge, winter sunset.
Canon 5D Mk II, 17-40mm f/L at 20mm, ISO 100, 157 seconds at f/16, LEE 4-stop ND and 0.6 hard grad.

Types of Lines

Diagonal lines tend to be dynamic, suggesting action and depth. Straight, converging lines are also dynamic, and can create a lot of impact but there is a danger the eye will be led out of the picture very quickly. Curves lack the immediate impact of diagonals or converging lines but 'S' curves in particular can be very effective for gently leading the eye around the whole picture, allowing the viewer to take in all the elements in the composition.

Horizontals are more relaxing than diagonals, suggesting peace and calm. Related to horizontal lines is the concept of layers which have the same tranquil properties, but can also help to enhance depth in a photograph.

Creating Depth

The world has three dimensions but a photograph has only two – poorly composed shots often appear flat. So how do we go about creating a sense of depth in a two-dimensional medium? Basically, by exploiting the same visual cues that the brain uses to interpret three dimensions from the image projected onto the retina.

Our eyes judge distance by using linear perspective. For example, we know railway tracks are parallel but they seem to converge and apparently diminish in size the further away they are. Likewise, we understand

The reflections of the sky in the rockpool help to tie things together in this shot. Middle Beach, Studland, August sunrise.
Canon 1Ds Mk II, 17-40mm f/4L at 21mm, ISO 100, 1/5 second at f/16, LEE 0.9 soft grad, polariser

that if there are two objects of a similar size, the one furthest away will appear smaller. If you compose a shot with a number of similar objects going away from the camera, such as a line of trees, you create a strong impression of depth.

The effects of linear perspective can be enhanced by choice of lens and viewpoint; by getting in close to the nearest object with a wide angle lens, the apparent distance between the foreground and more distant objects will be greater than if we shoot the same scene from further away with a telephoto lens. This is one reason foreground interest is key to many compositions.

While this is a powerful technique, it should be used with a degree of thought. Just using the nearest large rock as foreground interest, for example, won't necessarily deliver the best result. A good foreground is one which complements the background and links together the different planes in a composition. Look for foregrounds which help direct attention into the frame and which enhance the view in some way. 'U' and 'V' shapes for example, are useful for helping to frame the scene at the bottom of an image. Squares and rectangles, on the other hand, tend to block, and discourage the viewer from looking into the scene.

Other Compositional Tips

Layers

Look for lighting conditions which separate the planes in a scene into distinct layers. Side-lighting in landscapes with overlapping ranges of hills, or, misty or hazy conditions often create this look.

Pay Attention to the Sky

Keep an eye on the sky; if it is interesting, use it. Making the most of a strong sky can sometimes mean breaking the rules, for example, by placing the horizon very low in order for the sky to dominate the composition.

The Rule of Odds

This won't always be within your control, but if you have a several objects within your composition, such as a group of trees, odd numbers are more pleasing to the eye than even numbers. Three is the magic number.

Frames Within the Frame

This refers to the use of objects in the scene such as overhanging branches of trees to frame the view beyond. This helps by directing attention in towards the main subject and also helps create depth by separating the foreground plane from the background. To be more subtle with this technique, try using a partial frame rather than filling the top of the image.

The lamp post on Swanage's Victorian pier acts as a partial frame to this composition. Wide angle distortion has caused the bar below the lamp to angle downwards, so it subtly points towards one of the focal points – the man on the end of the pier, watching the sunrise. Pentax 67II, 45mm f/4, Fuji Velvia.

mark**bauer**
PHOTOGRAPHY

Biography

Mark is one of the UK's leading landscape photographers and photographic tutors. Having first become interested in photography while living abroad in the early 1990's, he is now renowned for his evocative images of Dorset and other locations throughout the south west of England.

As a professional photographer for over ten years he supplies images to stock agencies, corporate clients and magazines. He is a regular contributor to the UK photographic press, in particular *Amateur Photographer, Landscape Photography Magazine* and *Digital Photographer.*

Mark's work has been Commended and Highly Commended in various major competitions, including the International Landscape Photographer of the Year, the Landscape Photographer of the Year and the International Garden Photographer of the Year. In 2011 he was a category winner in the Outdoor Photographer of the Year competition.

This is Mark's fifth book. Previous publications include *Romantic Dorset* and *Perfect Wiltshire* and co-author (with Ross Hoddinott) of two photography technique books, *The Landscape Photography Workshop* and *The Art of Landscape Photography.*

Mark is lucky to live in the seaside town of Swanage with his wife Julie and their son Harry and has the many locations of Purbeck on his doorstep, quite literally.

Workshops and Tuition

As a former teacher and teacher trainer Mark has the skills to convey his in-depth knowledge of landscape photography to others. He is a co-owner of Dawn 2 Dusk Photography with Ross Hoddinott. Together with Adam Burton (author of Photographing Cornwall and Devon, published by fotoVUE), they run one day and residential photography workshops all over the UK (*www.dawn2duskphotography.co.uk*)

In addition to group workshops, Mark is available for one-to-one tuition which usually take place in Dorset, but can be arranged further afield.

Mark also works as a freelance tutor for others, leading workshops in many destinations around the world.

Visit Mark's website for more information:

www.markbauerphotography.com

Sunrise and ice on the beach at Jökulsárlón in South East Iceland. Canon 5Ds, 16-35mm f/4L at 16mm, ISO 200, 3.2 seconds at f/16, LEE 0.9 medium grad and 1.2 ND

Mark's photographic equipment

Canon 5Ds
Canon 16-35mm f/4L
Canon 24-70mm f/4L
Canon 70-300mm f/4-5.6L
Fuji X-Pro2

Fuji 10-24mm f/4
Fuji 18-55mm f/2.8
LEE Filters
Gitzo Ocean Systematic Series 2 tripod
Arca Swiss D4 head
F-Stop Satori bag with Large ICU

About fotoVUE

If you are a keen photographer or want to take the best photos when out and about or on holiday, **fotoVUE** guidebooks show you where and how to take photographs in the world's most beautiful places.

Website – *www.fotovue.com*

Visit our website for articles on how to improve your photography, view inspirational photographs and learn more about our guidebooks.

- Find out about our books
- Additional viewpoints
- Photography tutorials
- News and special offers
- Inspiration – full of amazing photographs
- Articles and features by leading photographers

Register for the fotoVUE newsletter to get regular updates and offers on our guidebooks.

Exisiting books

fotoVUE photographer-authors use their local knowledge to show you the best locations to photograph and the best times to visit.

- *The Lake District* – by Stuart Holmes
- *North Wales* – by Simon Kitchin
- *Wildlife in the UK* – by Andrew Marshall
- *Cornwall and Devon* – by Adam Burton

Buy from **fotovue.com**, Amazon, Waterstones, bookshops and direct from the authors.

Forthcoming Titles

- *Photographing the Dolomites* – James Rushforth
- *Photographing the Peak District* – Chris Gilbert, Villager Jim and Mick Ryan
- *Photographing Scotland* – Dougie Cunningham
- *Photographing South Wales* – Drew Buckley
- *Photographing London* – George Johnson
- *Photographing the Yorkshire Dales* – Lizzie Shepherd and Oliver Wright
- *Photographing West Ireland* – Carsten Krieger
- *Photographing the Snowdonia Mountains* – Nick Livesey
- *Photographing Northumberland* – Anita Nicholson
- *Photographing East Anglia* – Justin Minns
- *Photographing the Cotswolds* – Sarah Howard
- *Photographing Iceland* – Geraldine Westrupp, Martin Sammtleben and James Rushforth

Check the website for the latest on release dates.

Upload your own
Photographs and Viewpoints at:

www.fotovue.com

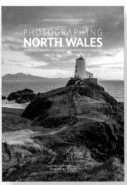
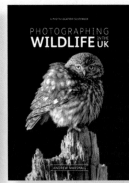

Opposite: From 'Photographing the Peak District' by Chris Gilbert, Villager Jim and Mick Ryan. Crow Stones, August sunset. Canon 6D, 17-40 at 27mm, ISO 100, 1/6 sec at f/14. © Chris Gilbert